THEY'RE PISTOLS AND They're Loaded!

A Mother and Daughter's Perspective on Life

Leilani Essary Hurles
& Lani Polasek

They're Pistols and They're Loaded!
A Mother and Daughter's Perspective on Life

Leilani Essary Hurles
www.LeilaniHurles.com or
www.TheyrePistolsandTheyreLoaded.com

Published by:
Aviva Publishing
Lake Placid, NY
518-523-1320
www.avivapubs.com

ISBN #978-1-938686-49-8

Editor: Tyler R. Tichelaar
Cartoonist: Sylvia Breece
Cover Design and Layout: Fusion Creative Works

Printed in the United States of America
First Edition

For additional copies visit:
www.TheyrePistolsandTheyreLoaded.com

Dedication

What makes a person write a book? Love, hate, sex, anger, dreams, or something else? I wrote my first book because after being diagnosed with ovarian cancer, I felt I needed to express myself in a way that would benefit others. After great thought, I decided to write another book along with my daughter Lani. This time, the love of life and sense of humor that carried me through the last three years that God graciously gave me, and a wonderful daughter who stuck with me through thick and thin, inspired me to tell her just how much she kept me going. So here we are embarking on the threshold of a new adventure. With the Lord as our guide, Lani and I hope that you too enjoy the fun we have together. We dedicate this book to "Our Magoo"...my dad, Lani's granddad, and also a great-granddad, uncle, great-uncle, friend, and just an incredible person.

Dad passed away February 6, 2013 at the age of ninety-eight. He was an Eagle Scout, a pilot decorated as an Army Captain with the Silver Star and Purple Heart in World War II. Dad was a Shriner, a Master Mason, the last living charter member of Lakeside Country Club, and the founder of Big Brothers Big Sisters in Houston.

We will miss you, Dad. We love you dearly. The material you provided me for my books was a gift you did not even know you were giving. And I know all the Magoo fans out there will remember all my dad's antics and laugh at all the havoc he is creating in Heaven. HUGS, DAD!

Acknowledgments

To the people who have touched our lives and to those who will in the future, thank you. Life is full of surprises, and we are thankful for the time you have and will spend with us.

To the doctors we share: Dr. Michael Bevers, Dr. Paul I. Cook, Dr. Mark Bing, Dr. Anil Odhav, Dr. Timothy Sehorn, Dr. Adam Czelusta, Dr. Robert Parker, and Dr. Ryan Ahern—you are the best at what you do and the nicest. Our family is forever grateful that God put you in our lives and has blessed you with amazing lifesaving skills. Our family thanks you for your ability to put up with both of us because we know it can't be easy. Your encouragement never takes a vacation. We love you!

And to our friends whose support never ceases. Lani's life friends who help her through thick and thin, childhood friendships that have lasted decades, neighbors who are always willing to help, new friends who are there when we need them, and to Linda and David Harris, who never cease to amaze us with their unconditional love.

Table of Contents

Preface	9
Introduction	11
Just a Thought	15
Ho-Ho-Hoing	25
Stick It in Your Back Pocket	39
Cowgirl Up	53
Incidentally Magoo	67
Dogs, Horses, Snakes, Oh My!	85
Magoo, Moms & Medicine	99
Magoo & Bill Strike Again!	113
Life without Lani	131
Family Photo's	145
The Hanging Boob Box	153
Copperhead Chaos!	165
Magoo on the Loose	169
Men on Duty	189
God Calls Us All Home	205
Getting It Off Your Chest	217
We Have Lost Magoo	235
Put Me in Coach	249
Adventures End and New Ones Begin	261
Leilani's Life Lessons	263
A Giving Thought	267
Information on Ovarian Cancer	271
Signs and Symptoms	

Foods for Thought and Downright Good!	275
Michele Joy Polasek Recipes	277
Linda Harris Recipes	279
Patsie Lockett Recipes	283
Zammitti's Italian Ristorante Marinara Sauce	285
Joe's Pinto Beans	287
The Perfect Baked Potato	289
Shrimp-and-Okra Hush Puppies	291
About the Authors	293

Preface

They're Pistols and They're Loaded is a humorous look at an incredible mother and daughter relationship, written as a collection of Leilani's Monday blog updates (written at her website **www.RideBabyRideBook.com**) about her battle with ovarian cancer as well as the antics of her family and friends, and through it all, Leilani has been by her side. Leilani and Lani are two peas in a pod, Pete and Repeat. They are energetic and unpredictable, and they never give up hope that they will have many more days together. This book reveals their situations of strength and courage and knowing that they are there for each other. Thrown in are fantastic recipes from family and friends, tidbits on life, photos, and a bunch of other fun stuff.

After Leilani was diagnosed in 2010 with stage 3 metastatic ovarian cancer, Leilani and Lani entered a love and friendship that only a mother and daughter can feel. It is through this inseparable relationship, which started with Lani's birth in 1979 and continues today, that true unconditional love of life is lived.

The girls hope you will love each other and live life to its fullest. In the movie *Auntie Mame*, the character Mame Dennis says, "Life is a banquet and most poor suckers are starving to death!" Get the picture? Leilani and Lani do, and they are loaded for adventure.

Introduction

Never Did Anything We Couldn't Get Ourselves Out of... Yet!

When you put the two of us together, something's going to happen. Maybe because we are experts at finding trouble. No, trouble doesn't find us. We find it. Lani and I have always been close, but I didn't realize how close until I was diagnosed with ovarian cancer in January of 2010—the most horrible day of my life, besides the passing of my beautiful mother. Through it all, Lani has been a daughter, friend, partner-in-crime, laugh-mate, inseparable, and whatever else God threw in there for the two of us. We are pals!

When Lani and I are ready to go, both barrels are loaded for fun. But…for real, no jail time or NOTHING! Sounds boring, doesn't it? Well, believe me, it's not. It's been a blast! As far back as I can remember, Lani and I have been sidekicks. My two boys were into baseball and football with their dad who coached their teams. Lani and I would find things to keep us busy. Between the two of us and my mother, we could always find an establishment that needed our business. Shopping comes naturally to the family. (My mom was one of Houston's original Sakowitz store's models). Anything and everything was up for discussion.

There is a story my cousin tells of when my mom and she used to go shopping and hide different outfits in each other's closets and tell my dad and my cousin-in-law that they belonged to another relative. I can just hear them and the BS now.

Lani and I have slept overnight on the train car "City of New Orleans." We have gone on several cruises together. We have dined in some of the most incredible restaurants, and we have met some of the most influential people. And we have wet our pants more times than we can count by laughing our asses off. I wish you could actually do that…I could really lose the weight.

On a Caribbean cruise, we decided that the way to meet people (while Bill was doing his thing in the casinos) was to hit the bars on board. Strolling the different decks, we hit upon a club that played all '50s and '60s music. The band was from The Philippines, but the lead singer sounded like any artist that he impersonated, especially Elvis. But just try to hold a normal conversation with the band members...you couldn't understand one word they said. Our new friends introduced us to the celebs on board, and at closing…about 3 a.m....we would head to the pizza place and get a pizza to go. Get back to our cabin and watch Dick Dastardly and Muttley. Yes, and wet our pants!

If you read the first book *Ride, Baby, Ride!*, you know about the time we locked the keys in the Jeep and had to push Lani's butt through the unzipped window to open the door. Not only did I have one accident, but two.

The Alley Theater and TUTS (Theater Under The Stars) are two of our favorite hangouts. We love going to the plays and musicals at least four times a year. This last trip was to see *The Best Little Whorehouse in Texas*. The wine flows freely and so does the laughter. "Fruit of the Loom" makes a fortune off of us.

In writing this book, I thought of things I would like for Lani to know—things she could use when I was gone. A "how to get along without me" type book. So here it is—our joint effort to keep us going no matter what crap life throws at us. So have your catcher's mitt on and throw it right back.

WE'RE PISTOLS AND WE'RE LOADED!

Just a Thought

Website Launched!

November 7, 2011

We have just launched the *Ride, Baby, Ride!* book website! Thanks for visiting!

About Monday Updates

November 10, 2011

Hello, Everyone…thanks for stopping by.

Thought I would take a minute, a deep breath, and I probably should grab a glass of wine…to pass on what you can expect from this website. Ovarian cancer has been an unbelievable shock. No one really can grasp the anger, fear, love, hate, and other emotions that go through your mind when something life-threatening enters your life. It appears out of nowhere, and in my case, will be with me the rest of my life. Okay…so be it. There is one thing you all must know from the beginning…Leilani does not give up. So, every Monday, and at other times during the week, I will post a Monday Update. These updates are full of information and real life happenings that occur in my world. Please feel free to comment and become a part of our fight to beat ovarian cancer.

Ride, Baby, Ride!

Don't forget to tell your friends!

November 13, 2011

Hey Everyone,

Don't forget to tell your friends to be sure and check in every Monday. My Monday Update will now be posted on the website rather than sent as an e-mail. However, I will e-mail all you "regulars" to remind you of the change the first couple of Mondays.

Hugs,

Monday Update

November 14, 2011

Hi Everyone,

Sometimes family members are forced to spend more time together than they care to, like during chemo week. The chemo victim is scared to go anywhere too far from base because you might make a total ass out of yourself. (Not me, of course; I could and would never make an ass out of myself! (LOL! Quit laughing.) I compare going out during the few days after chemo to a self-inflicted wound. Pointless! Anyway, so much closeness causes loved ones to rub each other the wrong way. I actually was ridiculed last week for the way I prepare my cereal. In sixty years, no one has ever made fun of my morning rituals…until now.

I'm not big on milk, sugar, and cereal for that matter. So not being a big cereal eater, when I do decide to hit the cardboard box, I have to mix my cereals. Yes, I am a cereal mixer! General Mills and Kellogg's should hire me. I come up with the best mixtures. It's not a handed down family recipe…it is a creation of cravings that my body signals to me. Experts say your body tells you what it needs. As a kid, I was a Rice Krispies fan. Snap, Crackle, and Pop were my dudes. My box heroes. But if your body is screaming Frosted Flakes that day…go find Tony. If your body says, "I feel like sitting in the 'john' all day"… go for the bran. Being a "practical Pete," go for the whole grain and so on. But don't ask me why anyone's system would ask for Cap'n Crunch. (Captain Morgan's a different story.) So…I mix my Fiber One Shredded Wheat squares to my whole grain Raisin Nut Bran. Thank goodness I do not eat cereal very often. A family member, who will remain anonymous, has now found another place to store his cereal. (Hint, he wears hearing aids and I'm married to him!)

I can honestly say the only good thing about the week after chemo is you don't have to worry about waking up with "bed head"! You just have to make sure your head is not permanently stuck to your pillowcase. Silk cases do help, but they are not foolproof. I am going to add to my increasing "bucket list" to find a perfect pillowcase for bald people. Oh yeah, and the perfect cereal blend!

I finally got over the achy bones and muscles from the white blood cell shot. But I have had a little shortness of breath while overexerting myself too much. Probably the red cells this time. It's always something. Sounds like an abundance of red meat this week to make up for it. Gee…a nice steak every day. See…there is a bright side to everything!

I want to close by thanking everyone for your continuous support of the book. The first week blew me away. I could not absorb all the kindness and love. Please encourage your friends to check the website for news and updates. We can all make a difference by inspiring those who need help and showing that they can depend on us. I plan on making a difference one book at a time.

Ride, Baby, Ride!

Just a Thought

November 18, 2011

Some days, I wake up with these incredible, earth-shattering points of wisdom! This morning, I started thinking about some of the people around me (especially the female ones) who are ready and eager to come to the aid and rescue of others, but they don't ask for a little help themselves. I decided that everyone should have a "go to" buddy, a chemo pal, an ace in the hole, etc. This person is chosen with the promise that he or she will listen to you at least once a day on anything you want to talk about. You need a listener, not someone rattling off unwanted advice, and not a family member. Family members get to hear you gripe and b-i-...tch all the time. This is your special person who at the end of your thoughts, fears, and plans, simply says, "Great. Have a nice day!" I have considered my "go to pal" as an extremely easy-going, non-excitable treasure in my life. As a matter of fact...I have several. How lucky is that? This need, my friends, does not just apply to cancer but to any adversity we might be facing. Life is short.

Ride, Baby, Ride!

Monday Update

November 21, 2011

Hi Everyone,

I would like to start today by telling everyone that I had the BRCA 1 & 2 test run. My doctor called me and I have tested positive for carrying the gene to pass ovarian cancer on to my children. But I also have the mutated BRCA 2 gene that puts me at high risk for breast cancer. I really don't know all the details yet. I have an appointment with Dr. Bevers after Thanksgiving so we can discuss all my options. Of course, I am more concerned about Lani and how she takes all of this. I am thankful, though, that we do have these tests that we can use to prevent future family cancer occurrences. Modern medicine is amazing. The BRCA test used to be done by blood testing, but now it is a very simple swishing of Scope first thing in the morning and spitting in a test tube. I know…how vivid? So, if anyone is worried about passing the cancer gene on, please look into this test. Insurance is the "iffy" part here. Need to see what criteria you need to meet for your particular insurance.

I'm sure everyone knows what a "bucket list" is. But just in case…it is a wish list of sorts…of things you want to do before you kick the bucket! I have decided that since everyone and his dog has seen me naked and my "who-ha" exposed, that I would like all the doctors, nurses, and techs, who got to view me while I was out cold, to line up and drop the scrubs! Sounds only fair to me. Hey, I might be missing something important! Some earth-scattering discovery. Leave out the female doctors, nurses, and the janitors, though. Not going there.

Okay, and I have added to the "things that drive me crazy" list. Have you seen the commercial where the V-8 juice dude jumps from some undisclosed place and scares the bejesus out of someone and then pours the person a V-8 fusion? Or the opera singers on the bus singing in their costumes for J.G. Wentworth? Or the Stanley Steamer guy on the floor, hugging it and smelling where some animal did his business? I'm telling you this world has gone nuts. REALLY! I'm starting to feel halfway normal having ovarian cancer.

I have found out that if you want to keep the mosquitoes away, go have a round of chemo. Now this is not scientific fact, but I can tell you that mosquitoes love me. I am bit constantly when they are out and about. But after chemo, they do not come near me. Go figure. I do notice that right before my next chemo, they start buzzing around again. I'm guessing because the chemo is starting to wear off and I need another juicing! Don't laugh; it's not chemo fog; it's just my normal crazy brain at work!

Bill and I had coffee with a good friend of ours, Ron, and his mother Phyllis, who was in from Bourbonnais, a little town south of Chicago. We met at Starbucks for coffee and had a great visit. Phyllis is a twenty-year breast cancer survivor and we bonded immediately on all kinds of topics from chemo fog to forgetting your modesty. My wish one day is that ovarian cancer survivors can say "I made it twenty, thirty, or forty years!" And we will! Anyway, I just want to get away from the negative and let's get to the positive. I get with my "pray pal," GOD, several times a day and we talk over finding a cure for cancer. Get'er done!

The book has really taken off. Lots of positive feedback. Remember $5 of each book goes to ovarian cancer research. So pass the word. Sending everyone a shout out for a WONDERFUL THANKSGIVING. I hope everyone has a blessed time with those who are with you, and I give thanks every day that I have friends and followers like you to keep me going. I am truly blessed!

Ride, Baby, Ride!

Happy Thanksgiving

November 24, 2011

May God bless all of you and your families during this season of thanks and love. We are so blessed to have each other.

Ride, Baby, Ride!

Monday Update

November 28, 2011

Good Morning All,

Hope everyone had a wonderful and safe Thanksgiving. We had a house full of family, food, and fun! The weather was gorgeous. Kids played lacrosse and ran amuck while the "big kids" (you know, the ones over twenty-one, thirty-one, oh hell, forty-one) attempted to played football. And everyone played guitars and sang on the back porch.

Believe me, this family can jam! The guitar players did an awesome job, but I have to say, the rest of us who tried to chime in, fell short!

With the weather getting cooler, a lot of us have started wearing scarves. Let me give you a peek into the life and times of Leilani's scarf. First thing is if you plan on being reincarnated as a scarf, do not come back as the end part. Either end. The part with the fringe. In one day's time, my scarf had been dragged on the floor, dropped in my food, caught in the car door, closed in the refrigerator door, sat on, almost strangled me, zipped up in my pants (don't ask), and dipped in the toilet! It's almost as bad as coming back as a pair of underwear, a toilet bowl, or a condom. Nothing that one would want to volunteer for.

All the Thanksgiving stuff has been put away and the Christmas decorations have emerged. Now all I have to do is worry about Bill falling off a ladder. Egad! You remember my Santa…wears red, hearing aids, ball cap, and men's Depends cup…let's not add broken leg to it.

Okay, busy week ahead. Blood work and exam with Dr. Bevers on Wednesday (where, I might add, that spreading the legs isn't so bad!). Ovarian Cancer Survivors Course on Thursday at MD Anderson. Lots of information on OC will be presented, including by Dr. Bevers' wife, Diane, who is also an OB/GYN Oncologist at MD Anderson. I will have a table set up to promote my book, which I hope will raise lots of money for MD Anderson OC research. And last but not least…chemo on Friday. Last one in this round! Bring out the wine! Let's hope I don't have to worry about it for a long time. And, of course, that's where your "knee-mails" come in. Please continue to pray for me and all of those who need our thoughts every day.

Ride, Baby, Ride!

Ho-Ho-Hoing

Well, I'll be darned. I've been looking for that toaster all week!
Hey! Is that my power drill?

December 3, 2011

Good News Everyone,

Chemo #6 came and went without a hitch. Now I have a PET scan scheduled after Christmas to make sure no cancer was left behind. Fighting a small headache but taking my nausea pills religiously. Keep prayers coming for great results.

The ovarian cancer conference was awesome. MD Anderson did a wonderful job and so did the Foundation for Women's Cancers. I gave out many business cards and donated a book to the MD Anderson Library. Talked to many cancer survivors who, as I do, fight for their lives every day. I couldn't sell books there because they are non-profit, but I had a mailing list for people who wished to buy.

Hope everyone has a great weekend. Go Texans! Beat Atlanta! And Go Houston Cougars! Beat S. Miss. This will give the Coogs the conference championship and go to 13-0! Awesome!

Ride, Baby, Ride!

December 5, 2011

Hi Everyone!

Feels like winter today. Finally! Usually Houston doesn't get a cool front until January. But we did get some much needed rain. Only bad part about it blowing in now is that I have to receive my white cell injection today.

Lani and I have a brilliant plan to keep Magoo occupied. Lani's friend TJ has a ninety-year-old grandmother who lives close to us. Only setback for her is that she can't hear. The only setback for Dad is he can't see. Now two setbacks can make a perfect match. And guess what? She has her own teeth too. Will wonders never cease? They can go on dates to the dentist. Plans are in the works. The only question is who would kill who first.

After chemo Friday, I had a "low key" weekend. Perched myself in my chaise lounge with my blankets, pillows, and laptop. All bundled up. I even shared my perfect hideaway with my Lab, Starr. There were no major problems from chemo, and I took my awful drink to keep me from being constipated…so all in all, a pretty good chemo weekend. Now I can enjoy the wonderful Christmas holidays and concentrate on my family and friends. No more chemo! Stay positive!

Lani and I have planned a couple of shopping days and also a couple of girls' nights out. We have tickets to see the musical *White Christmas* and also our annual night at the Alley to see *A Christmas Carol.* Our mall trips are always full of excitement and mischief. Bill does not like malling with the girls…and the girls do not like malling with him! Talk about Scrooge! Just leave me and my

American Express card alone! And of course, Lani instigates all the trouble...I'm just an innocent bystander. Hey, how much trouble can an old bald-headed woman get into? Prospects are endless!

So, my friends, have a great week. I appreciate everyone's prayers that are sent. Please know that they are right back at ya! Special shout out to my friend Lindsay Bevers (Dr. Bevers and his wife Dr. Bodurka's eleven-year-old daughter). Lindsay wants to write her own book. I know that she will be successful. After all, she is the product of two very special, caring people. Not to mention my friend.

Hugs from Fulshear,

Ride, Baby, Ride!

December 7, 2011

Patrick Snow is a major force in my life. Full of enthusiasm and encouragement. Patrick is my coach and friend. He was instrumental in writing my book. Patrick is an author, keynote speaker, and entrepreneur. Please check out his website at **www.PatrickSnow.com**

December 9, 2011

Good Morning Everyone,

What makes life special? FRIENDS! Old and new friends.

Last night was amazing. Big Brothers Big Sisters had a get-together last night at Neiman's at the Houston Galleria. I met so many wonderful people who give of their time to help others. Signing the books for them was nothing but pure pleasure. I now have so many new friends that I can add to my blessings of old friends. My husband Bill and daughter Lani were my escorts, for moral support, and they were overwhelmed by the hospitality given to them as well. BBBS president Ron Hadley is awesome, so if anyone would like to become a BBBS to a kiddo in the Houston area or make a donation to this wonderful network of the "unselfish giving of time," please give them a call.

Thanks to my friends who sent e-mails and texts to wish me luck and give encouragement. You all hold a very special place in my heart.

Ride, Baby, Ride!

December 12, 2011

Getting more in the Christmas spirit each day. I love Christmas! It's by far my most favorite time of year. I strongly believe you get out of Christmas what you put into it. As a kid, I remember the things my parents did for my brother and me to make Christmas so special. The excitement of getting to stay up late on Christmas Eve was a huge treat. (I figured out after becoming a parent that this is all strategy. Let the kids stay up…wearing themselves out trying to hold out to see Santa....Then they will hopefully sleep a little later on Christmas morning. May work for most kids, but not for my middle child, Casey. Casey ran circles around Santa, his elves, his reindeer, and his parents!)

On Christmas Eve afternoon, we would start out by delivering gifts to friends and family. After it got dark, Mom and Dad would grab their "Christmas cheer" (a cocktail...usually Scotch), and we would roam the streets looking at the beautiful lights and decorations. The only two Santas in Houston to visit back in the early '50s, since there were no malls, were either the Santa at Foley's downtown or the Santa at Mrs. Baird's Bakery. The one at Mrs. Baird's always seemed to have more spunk. He sat in his sleigh with all the reindeer in front and had to drink "something" to keep him warm. Hence, the spunk part! The Foley's Santa was inside where it was warm.

Getting home from our annual adventure, Mom would have us all dress in our red flannel pajamas. Yes, they all matched! We were, as they say, in "elf land"...identical! Mother even went so far as getting matching house shoes, at least one of which my brother would always lose. Very clever on his part not to have to wear them. We looked like Santa's "throwback" elves.

The movies and TV shows I treasure at this time of year are *White Christmas* with Bing Crosby, the original

Miracle on 34th Street with Natalie Wood, the cartoon version of *Rudolph the Red-Nosed Reindeer* with Burl Ives narrating, and of course, our family cookie night favorite *Christmas Vacation*.

As I mentioned in last Monday's update, Lani and I have a couple of outings planned in the next two weeks. Our annual visit to the Alley to see *A Christmas Carol* and to TUT's to see the musical *White Christmas*. This is the first time I will see *White Christmas*. I'm sure it will be wonderful.

Enjoying getting rid of the chemo fog. Every day I feel stronger and ready to get my life back on track. I appreciate you hanging with me and letting me reminiscence about Christmas past. My wish is that we all have many more wonderful Christmas Eves together, and that we do not forget the love in giving. Remember, each morning is a joyous sunrise gift from God. Expect great things!

Ride, Baby, Ride!

December 16, 2011

Hi Everyone,

Lani and I would like to report on our excursion to the musical *White Christmas*. It was performed at Hobby Center in the Theater District in downtown Houston. It was awesome! If anyone needs a lift to make it through the holidays...this is your place to be. Totally entertaining from start to finish and, just like the original movie starring Bing Crosby, you are ready to count your blessings instead of sheep. I know that I have so many things to be thankful for this Christmas, and first on my list is being alive and treasuring each day.

Ride, Baby, Ride!

December 19, 2011

Good Morning,

Well, here we are the week before Christmas. Christmas shopping for the "right" gift for each person on my list. Although almost everyone has his or her likes and dislikes, which makes the Christmas ho-ho'ing a little easier, Dad (Magoo) is the exception to almost every rule. First of all, at age ninety-seven, he has everything. And if he wanted something, he would have us go out and buy it for him. So, what do you get Magoo? We thought about acting lessons, only because his academy award performances aren't very convincing. He pulled a humdinger with Lani yesterday. Bill, my brother, my nephew Walker, and I went to the (very disappointing) Texan game. Lani and her "football friends" had the privilege of dad-sitting. (Privilege here is used very sarcastically.) If they had been on a ship....he would have been dangling overboard! He did everything and anything to disrupt their fun. Then when I got home, he acted like nothing had ever happened. Watch out Hollywood...here comes Magoo!

Bill is bugging me for a list of things I'd like for Christmas. A new roll of duct tape would be helpful! (I think Lani used what I had left on dad yesterday.) First of all, I really don't need anything. I would love a little moped to scoot around Fulshear Farms on. And I would love a wetsuit so I could swim in the winter. (Dr. Bevers would probably kill me.) Have you ever sent any man…on purpose… to buy you anything? I just tell Bill "I'll love whatever you get me…just save the receipt!" OMG! Can't wait for Christmas morning. I think I'll just tell him to stick to Spec's Wines…their Merlot section. Now there's a gift never wasted. And a thank you to Linda and David for my Merlot-toting Santa…it is awesome!

Time also for me to get ready for a PET scan right after Christmas to see how well the chemo worked. God says a heart does not whine or rebel when things get tough. He musters the courage in us to trust Him in hard times. "In quietness and trust is your strength." So, with a new year comes new trust and faith. So off to war I go again in hopes of finding new ways to fight cancer. Thanks again for everyone's support with the book. Together, we can spread hope to others. So as we say in Texas…Merry Christmas, y'all!

Hugs and kisses under the mistletoe,

Ride, Baby, Ride!

December 24, 2011

Merry Christmas Everyone,

From the Hurles family to yours...we wish you a Merry Christmas and hope Santa brings you everything you want. It was so easy for me to tell Santa what I wanted. The last two years I have asked for one thing...to wake up each morning and love those around me. Each day is a blessing, and I will never take that for granted.

Today in Houston it is cool and wet...a perfect day to light the fireplace and enjoy the family. Lani and I plan on nesting in the kitchen today and cooking Christmas Eve dinner. The family should be over tonight to celebrate the joy of giving on Christ's birthday. Turkey, cornbread dressing, green bean casserole, giblet gravy, and of course, an assortment of desserts will be on the menu. The Honey Baked ham is always an added treat. The Honey Baked Ham Store always takes that burden off the cook. Thank you! My sis-in-law Libby is fixing the mashed potatoes and deviled eggs. When she sets the plates of eggs down, the girls just move out of the way... it's a major stampede. We three women have come to the decision that if we could set the plates outside, we could clear the house out for a little while.

Bill has done it again. Being the wonderful husband that he is...he asked me what I wanted for Christmas. And you women know what I'm getting at! Trying to play it safe, I just said, "How about clothes?" Which I really don't need, but I figured they were the safest items to let him pick out. Always amazed and surprised by men's taste...I am just holding my breath until Christmas morning. Oh God, please let it be something normal. (One year it was PJs with penguins on them...with built-in feet, flannel, hoodie, and, and, and...the most unusual color I've ever seen.) And, of course, I always tell him to keep the receipts.

So have a great weekend and I'll send the update on Monday. The neighbors will know how the gift thing works out. Bill might be duct-taped to the mailbox for pick-up on Monday.

Hugs to you all,

December 26, 2011

Good morning and hope no one has a Christmas "hang-over." I do not mean from drinking either. I mean from not going berserk. Trying to stay sane...with shopping and crazy people out in masses. Not only in the stores, but in the parking lots and on the roads. Bill and I were driving down Chimney Rock (a major street in Houston) and some "driving challenged" woman was headed straight for us. I guess she decided that her side of the road was too busy. She swerved back in about two car-lengths in front of us, almost side-swiping a poor driver in his Mercedes. Of course, Bill didn't have *enough* to say about women drivers. I wish his mouth worked like his ears!

Even before my two rounds of chemo, my two little toes' nails were almost nonexistent. Lani and Bill get a big kick out of teasing me about my little toes' nails. Well, I received a pair of Christmas socks and was putting them on when, to my surprise, my left little toe got its nail caught in the sock. Now, I have noticed that going through chemo, my nails have grown faster than usual. To me, this is kinda crazy because chemo is supposed to kill bad cells as well as some good ones (like one's hair). When I clip my toenails, I hardly ever had to clip the little one. Are you ready for this…it ripped the sock! I was so proud of myself! Bill and Lani were beside themselves. It's amazing how just the smallest things keep them amused. Lani wet her pants and Bill had to change his "Kotex" (male Depends diapers…still having to wear them since his surgery, but he should be off "the rag" soon)! It so nice that I can spread holiday cheer by just putting on my socks!

How about Christmas gifts? Anyone exchanging anything? Or just keeping them to "re-gift" when the occasion is called for? My mother was the master of "re-gifting." She would keep records with each unwanted gift and then redistribute for birthdays and future Christmases, knowing who gave it to her and whom she could give it to…that the person who gave it to her wouldn't be present at the time of the second unwrapping. I'm telling you she had it down to a science. I actually loved all my gifts this year. I'm extremely proud of Bill for not giving anything in the "dumb-looking," not wearable in public, non-fitting, colors from hell or re-gifting categories. I think enough hints were dropped and catalogs left on tables, opened to pages with circled items and sizes highlighted, that he could actually figure it out. Even a remote-toting, beer-can-holding hand could pick up the paper trail and get it right! OMG there is hope for men.

We gave our friends Linda and David an outdoor camera. The kind at Bass Pro that takes pictures at night of things in your yard. Linda cracked me up. As of the first day, two pictures have been taken. Neither one of a backyard critter. Linda forgot it was up and it shot pictures of her "little ass" going back and forth. They had been having trouble with something knocking down a bird feeder in their backyard. They would put it up, and the next morning, it was down again. Their property is backed up to a game reserve so it could be anything. Glad we didn't buy ourselves one. I could get into so much trouble with something like that.

Hope everyone has a great week. PET scan on Wednesday…I'll keep you posted. Happy New Year to all, and I hope that your 2012 is blessed with good health, friendship, love, and for our world…a cure for cancer.

Peace and hugs,

Ride, Baby, Ride!

December 29, 2011

Hi Everyone!

Had my PET scan yesterday. I guess I will not get my results until Wednesday when I see Dr. Bevers. I should get blood work results back at the same time. Each time I have a scan, it seems like the "stupid tube" gets smaller. I was almost claustrophobic this time. I wonder if the tech had my pillow too high or if I'm just gaining too much weight. I'll blame it on the pillow. Kept hitting my elbows on the ceiling of that "thing" when it would move back and forth. I need to bring my poster of George Strait and stick it to the roof of that "sucker" and forget all about the scan. Can't be too close to my man George!

Hope everyone has a wonderful 2012. Stay out of trouble on New Year's Eve. We will be at the Texan game on New Year's Day…which means happy thoughts of totally kicking some Titan heinie!

Ride, Baby, Ride!

Stick It In Your Back Pocket

January 15, 2012

That's okay. We are a young team and will survive. Just like life…we are in it for LOVE OF THE GAME! Love you Texans…we still believe for next season. Got my tickets...baby!

Ride, Baby, Ride!

January 16, 2012

There comes a time in everyone's life when you'd just like a week to end and a new one to begin. This last week was like a satellite crossing the sky among all the stars. Mostly confused and not shining as brightly as the heavens around it. Definitely trying not to crash into anything. Starting at one horizon, passing through and disappearing on the opposite side of the universe. Giving a "high-five" to the moon as it hurried, temporarily hiding behind it, and then reemerging and finding itself again. Such were the trials of Leilani during the Friday the 13th week.

The chemo fog lifted at its usual time. But the nausea and light-headedness lingered a little longer than I would have liked. Not sure if it's due to the extra poisoning session or just my brain telling me "Here we go again." But then as with every chemo session, "THE CHALLENGE" showed up. Always a challenge to get your heart pumping, the body racing, and the mind thoroughly pissed off! The saga of the dreaded toilet seat! We change out the toilet seat often because of chemo. It is always clean, but in the chemo manuals, they suggest trading out seats after your chemo sessions are over. Okay, so be it. Now in the middle of the night…nature calls. I run into the bathroom, hurry to lower the PJ bottoms, and proceed to slide from one side of the john to the other and off into the magazine rack located on the floor. Let's see; how can I describe the crash? The toilet seat had become very loose…it slid with me. The crash sounded like the explosion of a fireworks factory. Moochie and Starr started barking, the toilet paper holder was in my hand, completely dismantled from the wall, the wet wipe container was underneath me…smashed, and the picture on the wall had fallen down into the bowl. (The picture is of red roses. It looked like I was trying to water them.) Are you ready…I know you already know….Bill didn't hear a thing! So I just left everything the way it was and waited for "Mr. Fix It" to rise and shine. I do not know which was louder, the actual crash or him making the discovery. That's one good way of getting an all new toilet room! FYI, the new seat is so comfy.

On Saturday for the first playoff games, we had a few friends over to watch, eat, drink, and have fun. Our good friends Linda and David, Mark and Patsy, and niece Allie, Dusty, Michele, Casey, Christina, Aunt Libby, and of course, my sidekick, Lani. Magoo came in and out. Mostly out, which was awesome! Mark and Dusty had the BBQ duties and everything was so good. Patsy made homemade salsa. (I'll get the recipe for everyone and post it…fresh and healthy.) It was really a great time for me. I had been so bored all week and really needed the family around me. (Our friends are our family, so I just include them as family.) Friends are people who are there for you when they'd rather be somewhere else. I treasure my time with them.

Lani and I have an appointment with Dr. Lu at MD Anderson tomorrow. I'm glad we are getting this part of the detective work done. Dr. Lu is a genetics expert with BRCA and will guide us on the things we need to do to help Lani dodge ovarian cancer in the future. I met Dr. Lu at the ovarian cancer conference in December and really like her. I'll keep all up-to-date on the progress.

So, my friends, have a great week and keep flying across that sky. And please feel free to contact me at anytime. I love hearing from you, and I really enjoy the time I spend with you.

Ride, Baby, Ride!

January 17, 2012

Lani and I had a wonderful visit with the great staff at MD Anderson today. Amanda Brandt (Genetic Counselor) and Dr. Karen Lu guided us through our next steps to understanding and making decisions on our future with ovarian cancer. It's simple but so complicated. I have a greater risk of developing breast cancer now with my BRCA 2 mutation. Lani will take the BRCA test, and she has a 50/50 chance of being negative. Just have to wait on the results to see how we go on with her treatments. As for me...I head into an MRI of the ta-tas and a mammogram every six months. I have several options. Take it as it comes, or have the breasts removed. I figure the ovarian cancer is recurring...no options on that...so take each day as it comes. I will always do what I feel is the best thing for me and my family. I'm pretty strong. I feel I will endure whatever happens; it's just putting the family through all of this that bothers me. So, my friends...keep the prayers coming and know that the Good Lord will guide me to the right decisions. Like right now...He's telling me to go have a glass of wine with my husband and CHILL!

Ride, Baby, Ride!

January 18, 2012

Hereditary Breast and Ovarian Cancer Syndrome Education Conference

Saturday, February 4, 2012

9:00 a.m.-3:00 p.m.

For Info please call 713-745-7391 or go to ccg@mdanderson.org

If you are an Ovarian Cancer survivor, there is a program you might be interested in. The program is called "Survivors Teaching Students: Saving Women's Lives." This program helps med students understand firsthand about ovarian cancer symptoms and risk factors so future physicians can diagnose the cancer earlier.

Please contact
GynOncCommunityRelations@mdanderson.org
or phone 713-792-2765

January 19, 2012

I know we all have our favorite things to eat. But Bill and I have run into something that is not only good for you but easy to make: salmon patties. But not just normal salmon patties. The HEB store near us has them premade, or you can buy your salmon and make them yourself. Chopped onions, bell peppers, chunks of low-fat cheese (any flavor you prefer), jalapeno (optional), celery, and anything you choose to add or take out. Pan cook it in olive oil. You can leave it in patty form or crumble it over a salad. It is heaven. And it is on my "foods to increase" list. Others on that list are five servings of veggies/fruits a day. More flax, olive oil, almonds, walnuts, avocados, whole grains, and lots of water. Of course, after five, the water turns to wine!

Anyway, just wanted to share my new discovery. Let me know if you try the salmon recipe. Gee, "I should have had a V8" is proving very true!

Hugs,

January 21, 2012

I would like to thank everyone for all the wonderful birthday wishes. It is amazing how many of you remembered. I know that Facebook helped a little bit, but it's the thought that counts. Love back to you all. I had a wonderful pre-birthday lunch with some childhood friends yesterday. Sharon and Cynthia DeGeorge and Lani and I met at Dekker's in Fulshear and had a good time reminiscing. The DeGeorge family lived next door to us from the time I was three until we moved to the Memorial area when I was seven. So thanks, Sharon and Cynthia, for a great lunch filled with love, hugs, and memories.

Bill is taking me to dinner tonight at Sullivan's Steakhouse. Can't wait to enjoy a wonderful evening together. For lunch, we are meeting our friends Linda and David at The Mason Jar. Lani is in charge of Magoo (Dad) for the whole day. I couldn't have asked for a better birthday gift.

So again, thanks to all of you. You have made this a very special birthday for me. I will never forget it.

Ride, Baby, Ride!

January 23, 2012

Good Morning, Everyone!

If you read my birthday blog, you know I had a wonderful day. In fact…it was a wonderful birthday weekend. Sullivan's Steakhouse was incredible, and I would recommend it to everyone who would love a nice steak dinner with very nice people. Yesterday was just a plain old spaghetti and meatballs day. My "starting-to-get-wide" butt was in my chaise lounge all day, watching the NFL playoff games. My sis-in-law Libby came over for a visit with presents—a beautiful Western decor cross, which I hung in our den, and other awesome gifts, including a pair of pink horse designed rain boots.

I caught Lani and Bill's CRUD! That's the only word for it. Not like a cold, but cough and chest congestion. They are on antibiotics, but I was afraid to take anything except Tylenol because I am not a doctor, and I was scared that if I took anything, it might not go hand-in-hand with my chemo drugs. So I'm toughing it out. Bill loves it because I don't have a voice (which he doesn't hear anyway…in my opinion), and he finds it amusing that I can't pop off at him and others when I feel the need. It is quite frustrating, actually. I feel that everyone should hear my quips at life on occasion. You guys aren't so lucky…I don't need a voice to type.

It seems like last week I was at the beck and call of Mother Nature. Bill was in the kitchen and heard a loud thump. He looked out on our back patio and a little bird had hit the window and was out cold. The sparrow was scooped up and I held it for about two minutes. I rubbed its little head as it was cupped in my hands. It looked up at me, and more than likely, I probably scared out what life was left in him. Bald, in PJs, and on a mission. Eventually, he spread his wings and then looked me right in the eyes, wrapped his little feet around my finger, and hung out for a while. We really didn't have too much to discuss. But when he was ready, he took off. It was awesome. I love the way God gets our attention.

Our Aussie mix Moochie has hair that sheds everywhere. There is this invention they advertise on TV that is called a Shed Pal. If anyone has tried it on a pet, would you let me know how it works? I was discussing the use of it with Moochie, who did not seem real thrilled by the prospect of being groomed with this thing. If I could read dog minds, I think he was probably saying, "Why don't you just chase me around the house with the Dirt Devil?" Although I'm open to any suggestions. I guess I'm jealous that he has hair and I don't!

Getting my body and mind ready for my next poisoning session on Friday. I am having lunch today with Lani and my old time friend Velma. Then on Wednesday, I have an appointment with Dr. Bevers and blood work. Thursday, I hope to meet a new friend who contacted me via my business card. She recently moved to Fulshear from Dallas. I love meeting new people, and I hope she gets settled in and finds many friends in our area. Then Friday is "get juiced up day"....This will be number two of three. So that means one more left. Getting pretty tired of chemo fog. Oh, well, not much one can do about that.

Hope everyone has a fantastic week. Don't forget to check out my blog a couple of times a week for news stuff and updates. Y'all keep me going. Hugs from Fulshear!

Ride, Baby, Ride!

January 26, 2012

Hi Everyone,

Went for my pre-chemo appt. yesterday and my blood work came back not so good. All fine except the platelet count (PLT CT). It has to be at least 100 and mine was 93. Don't quote me...but something like that. So chemo will be postponed until after Bill and I get back from our Las Vegas trip to see George Strait on Super Bowl weekend. If George can't make those platelets rise, nothing can. Everything happens for a reason, and I guess the Good Lord decided that waiting another week would be the best. But besides battling this "sinus crud," I feel great and am as feisty as ever. I appreciate everyone who contacted me and wished me good luck. Hopefully next time. Believe!

Hugs,

January 30, 2012

Well, we are getting ready to start February, aren't we? Wow, time sure travels fast these days. As you know by now, my chemo was postponed until after our Vegas trip. Had a Dr. Bevers appt. and blood work, which came back almost immediately a "No go." Platelet count too low. Anyway, was hoping to get chemo #2 out of the way and really look forward to #3 coming and going.

Bill and I are getting ready for the trip to Vegas for Super Bowl activities and to see my honey, George Strait. We are now having to play a game with Magoo (Dad). So we don't have to see one of his Academy Award-winning performances when we leave (which, I might add, always makes you feel like you're deserting the "ole fart"), we have decided to play his game on him. So this week, I feel like I will earn the Oscar for an actress in a lead role. I have been kissing his "behind" for days now. Throwing in how upset I am that chemo was delayed and how I deserve a break, to get away, time to forget about it all (which is all true), and just be me! I really have come up with some doozies. I know the voices in my head aren't real, but they really have some brilliant ideas! So we will see how all of this plays out when we leave Friday morning. Poor Lani and my sis-in-law Libby will be in charge, along with our friend and doctor, Mark Bing.

The dogs are getting a little ESP feeling that something big is about to enter their lives. When we get the suitcases out, they go into a tailspin. So we are trying to hide any clues that we are getting ready to leave them for a few days. I have literally been packing things in my closet so they can't see the evidence. I know…but I'm not crazy, just a limited edition! But animals are amazing and do have that incredible sense of knowing what you are thinking. The horses like when we leave; everyone babies them with extra carrots and apples. They hardly know Mom and Dad are gone. If only we could feed Magoo extra carrots and apples to keep him normal.

I have an appointment with the ta-tas specialist at MD Anderson when we get back. Since the BRCA 2 was positive for the gene mutation, I will have to go through a boob MRI and a mammogram each year—one or the other every six months. There is an option of removing the hooters before anything shows up or waiting to see what happens. I have not talked with Dr. Bevers about this yet, but I will when we return. I swear…the poor man is either messing with the who-ha or feeling the boobs. Don't get me started….I promised numerous people I would stay out of trouble until I got back from Vegas.

I will send a shout out on Thursday with last minute feelings and a Magoo update. Have a great week, and to our friends Linda and David, if we don't see you before you leave for your Australian cruise…have a blast!

Hugs!

January 31, 2012

Just a quick update. Daisy, one of Dr. Bevers' nurses, called me yesterday to tell me even though my platelets were low, my CA-125 (cancer antigen) was outstanding…less than 1. Needless to say, that really raised my spirits. So look out, Vegas; here I come! But please, keep my platelets in your prayers. Love you all!

Cowgirl Up

February 2, 2012

Just wanted to tell everyone that there will be no Monday Update this coming Monday. Bill and I leave for Vegas tomorrow morning and will not be back until Wednesday. As we were packing today, our paint horse Bud developed an abscess in his left front hoof. We called our dear friend and farrier Trini to the rescue. He will be babysitting our baby while we are gone. Meanwhile, Magoo has started his tailspin and is acting like a complete jerk! Lani will have her hands full for five days. Anyway, I will have a blast for everyone. So, lifting the wine glass to a toast to you all.

Ride, Baby, Ride!

February 9, 2012

Hello All,

Back from Vegas and totally rejuvenated! Had blood work done today with all the sweet ladies at St. Luke's lab. Came back a "go" for tomorrow's chemo. Had an appt. with Dr. Arun and her wonderful staff at MD Anderson to do some research regarding the BRCA 2 mutation. Dr. Arun is a breast cancer specialist and will make sure my ta-tas stay healthy.

And what can I say about Vegas. OMG! George Strait touched my hand twice. Yes, had to change my underwear. Twice! That'll teach me to wear underwear to

George Strait. Martina McBride was awesome too. She sang the song about cancer that left no dry eye in the house. Need to get that CD.

Bill had to be disciplined twice that I know of. I took a picture of him and "Betty Boobs" and another one of him losing money at blackjack while watching a pole dancer at the Tropicana. I mean…who folds on a blackjack! I knew I should have packed the duct tape. There are many more stories and so many nice people. At MGM Grand, we met a sweet lady named Pat (who bought a book… thanks, Pat); she was such an enjoyable person to chat with. Also there we met Glen and Jamie, who were so nice to us and got us in the front row to watch George. I owe them huge hugs for the time of my life. And our friend Allen who got us tickets. And thank you Tommy, who sent Bill and me pictures from the concert….Thank you so much; we will treasure them forever. Thank you, Vera, for taking such good care of us at breakfast every morning. We sure missed you on Wednesday morning when you had your well-deserved day off. Don, our ticket dude at Harrah's, what a nice guy you are. We look forward to seeing you on our next visit. Paul and Julie, Bridget and Misty…our Super Bowl buddies. What fun. You really get to know people when you have to hold seats for hours before the game. Tom, our bartender at Harrah's, thank you for giving us ole farts the attention you do. And to all the Keno girls, Cheryl and crew, thanks for encouraging us to gamble at breakfast—we loved every minute of it!

And leaving Vegas, we were in the airport bar where we ran into Rick the bartender and three other Texans, Greg, Donnie, and Chris. Imagine meeting Texans in a bar. All in all, a blast, and if I left anyone out…hang on, there is more to come.

So, chemo tomorrow and a chemo fog weekend. Let me hear from you. Love you all!

Ride, Baby, Ride!

February 11, 2012

Just an update on how chemo went. No rashes this time and no nausea thanks to the steroid drugs they give you. So I guess, add a few more pounds to this "ole heifer." One more to go…and maybe some of the puffy look will disappear. If not, Dr. Bevers and I are going to have a loonnnggggg discussion on the subject. I sent Bill to the Italian place on the corner by chemo to pick up lunch, and I had a huge spinach salad and some baked spaghetti. Had plenty left over for dinner. Knew I wouldn't feel like cooking. Had the typical first night of chemo though. No sleep…housework time. Finally, I took an hour snooze about 7 a.m. Then back at it again. Sent Bill to the store to keep him out of my hair...well, out of my bald head. Anyway…OUT! Three hours of peace. Well, almost. He called three times because he couldn't find stuff in the grocery store. On the third time, I said, "Doesn't anyone work at the grocery store anymore…

someone who knows where things are?" Reminds me of the time when I was still working that he called me to ask me where the mayo was in the fridge. I told him exactly. He called back because he still could not find it. When I got home, I opened the fridge door, and there it was right next to the milk where I said it was. Do you know he actually accused me of planting it there! He got out of the hospital three days later.

So, back to cleaning and cooking for the next few days. I know the tired part and foggy feeling is on its way. Talk to you all Monday on the update. Ran across a quote that I really liked from an unknown author. It goes like this: "Do what makes you happy. Be with who makes you smile. Laugh as much as you breathe. And love as long as you live."

Ride, Baby, Ride!

February 14, 2012

Hi All,

All went well at my white cell injection yesterday. Poured rain all the way there and back. Never fails when we have to hit the road for chemo or an appt. of some kind. Lani was my chauffeur since Bill was busy tending to the horses and the barn. We endured the rain and had lunch at Luby's Cafeteria and ran several errands.

Bill and I have heard from so many of you that we met on our trip. Bill played three-card poker with a very nice lady named Janet from Minnesota. I sat behind them in the cheering section since I am not much of a gambler. (I like video poker. Simple and easy to get up from if you start losing!) Anyway, we heard from Janet and from Julia, who was with a group of young ladies from Texas whom we sat next to at Wolfgang Puck's in the MGM Grand. By the way, best linguine and clams I have ever had.

Today will be a slow, relaxing day. Bones ache from the injection and lots to catch up on. Lani and I are going over ideas for our book, and we can't wait to get it started. Bill has been sent on more errands...should take him a few hours today. I think I'll take the phone off the hook. The boy needs to learn to fend for himself…right? I have several comments about males in grocery stores too. The funnies are endless. Go figure.

On Thursday, I have a mammogram scheduled. This is part of the BRCA testing trials stuff. Hopefully, all will go well and I won't have to worry about the ta-tas. I mean, how many body parts can one dispose of? Bill and I need to go back to Vegas to revisit Madame Tussauds' wax museum. In there, it is all pretend, so I could pretend I have a whole body again. Man, the figures they created in wax were remarkable. So real-looking. Even scary at times. I had my picture taken with one of my favorites:

Dean Martin and the Rat Pack. Awesome…Dean didn't care if I was missing parts!

I'll report more after Thursday's mammogram. Stick with me….I need those prayers to keep coming. You are my backbone, and friends are God's way of telling us we are loved.

Ride, Baby, Ride!

February 18, 2012

How fun are mammograms? I say this every time, but there has to be a better way. With all the new technology out there, you know there has to be some male behind them, getting revenge in some way for women naggers. Here is a woman (now a man doing this might give me a little dignity), but this woman, whom you've never met, manipulates your bazoomas for thirty minutes or so. Fully squashing, squeezing, squishing, clasping, flattening, deflating, compressing, clutching, and pinching the knockers so they feel like a Minute Maid orange does while being made into juice. So here I am stripped from the waist down, wig hanging on for dear life, and a hospital gown opened at the front. Now, why a gown? At one point, I had both "barrels" up there at the same time. And Yogi Bear nipple Band-Aids? Really? (What do you do for a living?…I manufacture nipple Band-Aids!) If I am going to wear a nipple Band-Aid, I want George Strait's picture on it. Anyway, I wanted to tell my breast cancer friends that I will have to do this twice a year from now on. One mammogram and one breast MRI. There is an option to remove the ta-tas to avoid breast cancer, which as you all know, I am at high risk of with the BRCA 2 positive mutation. But Dr. Bevers says to wait a while and let's fight this ovarian stuff first. I have come to the conclusion that women could avoid a whole lot of headaches if they would just have all female parts removed after the child-bearing business. I mean, Wow! I think I could have certainly lived without the reproductive parts, and the only person who would have been upset about losing the "hooters" would have been Bill. But I want to thank Jennifer, the tech, and Martha, the nurse, for being so sweet and trying to make it a good experience. Martha's niece just found out that she has stage 3 ovarian cancer. Please send prayers out to her. I am not sure of her name, but the Lord knows who you mean!

Looking forward to getting a new week started. Lots to do. Talked with my website guru, Tony, yesterday; he has added Facebook and is working on adding the sale of *Ride, Baby, Ride!* T-shirts to the site. Many of you have been asking me when they will be on the website for sale…so real soon. There is even a book/T-shirt deal if you get both. Thanks for all the support. We are slowly raising money for MD Anderson ovarian cancer research. I have a lunch date with Kristine from MD on Tuesday to get the money in MD's hands. I'll get everyone the info as it becomes available.

Hugs from Fulshear,

February 20, 2012

Good morning!

Had a pretty good weekend. Mostly inside due to rainy weather on Saturday and a cool but beautiful Sunday here in Houston. I updated quite a bit on Saturday. But I do have some new information for you.

My CA-125 came back a 2. So I am really excited about that. It was a 1 last time, but it can fluctuate a little each way, depending on where (meaning which lab does the calibrating) and who (which tech calibrates it). So as my nurses at Bevers' office tell me, I am doing really well. I am feeling a lot stronger now, which is normal after a week of pure hell right after chemo. It just takes time to recover from the body being poisoned every few weeks.

My son Dusty came over to help Bill do a few things around the property, and he was nice enough to shave off what fuzz I had left on my head. I was being ridiculed for looking like Karl Rove! No rest for the sick...the family is supposed to be supportive. Not on the floor laughing their asses off. OMG! It was true. Bald with fuzzy gray strands of hair sticking out all over my head. And if I put on my glasses with the "steroid-rounded face look"...I could have been his twin. Anyway...took care of that dilemma real quick.

Our little wren family is back and busy building its nest on our back porch in a hanging basket. They were singing and putting on a show this morning. Bill and I sat at the kitchen table, laughing and listening and watching all the commotion going on. Just watching the amazing energy God's creatures have gives me the energy to keep fighting. When the plethora of everyday problems seems to require more and more of our time and energy, that's when we need to step back and say, "Look at the wrens. God has given them the knowledge and strength to keep going. They trust Him." We need to know that God has also given us the knowledge and strength—we just need to ask for it and use it and trust Him. Meanwhile, the mockingbird family up by the front gate has been busy too. All kinds of stuff going on out there. Battles for territory and mates is always fun to watch.

Which brings me to my mate. Has anyone ever tried the earphones that they advertise on TV? The ones that amplify the speaker levels for the person wearing them. You plug this "thingy" in the receiver and the person can turn up the volume without bothering anyone else. Lani and I are looking for a pair of those headsets. Our den TV is on the wall that is shared with her bedroom and the headboard of her bed. When Bill is watching TV, she is dislodged from her bed and blown to Bermuda by the blast of airwaves. Heaven forbid the days she wakes up with a hangover. If you have tried these or know anyone who has...please let me know. I wonder whether mother mock or mother wren have the same problem.

Have a wonderful week. I will be adding new things every few days. I have lunch tomorrow with Kristine from MD Anderson to discuss the ovarian cancer research fund. I'll get the details of that to you. Really looking forward to getting things going. I have a check waiting for them. Thanks to all of you who have purchased books and have bought T-shirts. Please pass the word so that we can raise more money. Take care and Ride, Baby, Ride!

Hugs,

February 24, 2012

Well, the big rodeo is back in town, and I have heard that the cookoff last night was a blast. Wish I could have been there, but Lani is out of town for a few days and will be back Sunday evening. Visiting her boyfriend in South Carolina. I am so happy when she gets to get away from it all. She is such a trooper, and I can't imagine what I would have done without her. Anyway, hope everyone who goes to the cookoff this weekend has a couple of beers for me. And don't forget the food! Ride, Baby, Ride!

Bill and I leave for Oakland on Monday. Going on my train ride through the Sierras and then back to Oakland. I can't wait. I haven't slept on a train since I was a kid. I still remember how much I loved it. Riding through the

California and Nevada mountains ought to be awesome. Thanks to our doctor and friend Mark Bing who owns his own train car, "the Silver Iris," and was nice enough to share. If you go online and search for "Silver Iris," you can see what the train car looks like. My big feat coming up is to let Magoo (Dad) know we are leaving. I can only imagine what illness he will come up with. Poor Lani; she will be in charge. I have recruited several others to help. Libby (my sis-in-law) is house-sitting for our friends, Linda and David, so she is out of commission. It, no doubt, will take about four others to take her place. I will send a Monday Update before I leave and let everyone in on how Magoo takes the news! I hope there is a lot of wine on that train! I'm sure there will be...Mark knows me well!

Hugs,

February 27, 2012

"It was the best of times, it was the worst of times" or something like that. I should win the Academy Award! I outdid Magoo by a landslide! Mom, wife, teacher, coach, author, and now actress. I worked up to the big day to drop the announcement that we were leaving for our train trip until Friday morning. Each day, I dropped bigger and bigger hints until finally Friday morning, "the cat was out of the bag." So Magoo (Dad) counter-performed (it still amazes me how he does it and that he actually thinks it will work) on his "I'll get you for this, my little pretty, and your little dog, too!" This time… Dad informs us he can't hear. What happened…a land mine explosion? No, wax build-up. So he couldn't get away with anything, our friend and family doctor saw him in his office on Sunday. (Thanks, Mark for being such a saint.) He cleaned out Dad's ears. I have to admit that wax did come out, but about the amount to make a wax figure of an ant! We all teamed up so Dad had no excuse for ruining our trip. I still say he is over there in his adobe, scheming up something. We leave here for the airport about 11 a.m. Fingers and toes are crossed.

Oakland, here we come, and Silver Iris, here we come. I'll send updates if I can get to a computer this week. Otherwise, we will return home Tuesday week, and I will have all kinds of news for you. I'm sure Lani will have numerous tales too. Never a dull moment when she is dad-sitting Magoo. But I am so looking forward to getting away before my final chemo that is scheduled for when I return. Please pray for a safe trip…of course, we wake up this morning and the first thing we hear on Fox News is a train derailment in Ontario, Canada. Never fails, does it?

Love and hugs to you all.

Ride, Baby, Ride!

Incidentally Magoo

March 8, 2012

We're back! And the stories are endless. So I will start out with the flight to Oakland to catch the train and then go through each escapade from there…giving everyone a break in between.

The flight to Oakland was smooth, and we enjoyed meeting people who sat around us on the plane. We arrived in Oakland and took a cab to Emeryville where we checked into the Hyatt House. Our room overlooked the train station…so we had choo-choo trains going through all night, which I loved. The clickety-clack of the wheels was very soothing. We went down to the bar for drinks and dinner and met up with another train car mate, Dr. Clemis Jackson. (He is in the same offices with Dr. Mark Bing, who owns the train car). The next morning, we boarded the snow train. It had about fifteen cars (guessing…it was long). We were the first car behind the engines. And on the way to Reno, we were serenaded by ELVIS! Yes, Elvis was in the building, or in this case, "on board." Blue sequined suit and all. It was a hoot! On our way to Reno and climbing up to 5,000 feet, we experienced an unbelievable snowstorm. This Texas girl was so excited. I have never seen that much snow. When we arrived in Reno, we got off the train and hit the casinos. There were so many wonderful traveling companions in our car. Coni and Donna, Shelly and Jerome, Ann and Ken, Clemis, Alan, and our crew...Jan, Bob, and my friend Mark Bing. Thanks for making our trip so enjoyable....We had a blast!

First night on the train...now how do I describe hauling my fat ass up that tiny ladder to my upper berth sleep station? Well, it's better than Bill's butt falling out of the top bunk in the middle of the night. So he got the lower berth. You have to know this part. The entire cabin was about 10' long and about 6' wide. With suitcases and small table...that doesn't leave much room. Each room had a toilet and sink. This area was 3' by 3'. Talk about claustrophobic! Pooping in there was worse than being in the PET scan tube! During my next PET scan, I'll be laughing my rear off thinking about the train bathroom adventures. The second night on the train, I told Bill to move over. My body was not climbing that ladder again. The night before, I had my wig perched on the ceiling of the toilet along with my glass of wine. Hell, I wasn't going to come down for anything and have to go back up. Well, I gave in when I had to pee. But I cussed all the way down and back up. So the second night, Bill slept with his head at one end and mine at the other. Don't ask...a picture is worth a 1,000 words...and believe me, there is no Facebook floating pictures of that! The ride back was just as beautiful. Lots of snow until we came to the bottom of the mountains.

So ends the first part of our trip. Hope everyone has been well and has had a good week. We see Reba tomorrow at the rodeo. Can't wait for that. Have a great rest of the week and I'll be back tomorrow with more on the trip. Missed you all.

Ride, Baby, Ride!

March 10, 2012

Have no idea what happened to me. Dr. Bevers said I must have caught a "bug" probably on the plane or in some other tight quarters. Could not go to the Reba concert last night. And now glad I didn't with all the rain, wind, and chilly temperature. Instead, home in bed with 101 fever…coughing my head and chest off. Lani and Dusty (my daughter and son) went to Reba for Bill and me. I couldn't imagine giving up chute tickets. Still coughing this morning, and chest and throat are hurting…but I have to get well for chemo on Monday.

I need to pick up where I left off on the trip. So I will start with leaving Oakland. At the airport, we were getting ready to board our flight when the entire St. Mary's College basketball team shows up to get on the same plane headed for Vegas. They were playing in the Western Conference finals. Anyway, there were not enough seats. So Southwest was asking people to give up their seats and take a later flight. We volunteered, and in doing so, we received a voucher for $200 apiece in Southwest Airlines tickets. Then when that second flight was due to take off, they were asking for two seats because they had to get a crew somewhere else so we gave up our seats again. This time we received $400 each in Southwest Airline tickets. So now we are up to $1,200 between us. Lani said we should stay in Oakland...we were making more money than we would ever make in Vegas. She did have a point. Finally, we arrived in Vegas about 7:30 p.m. on Friday. We saw two great shows. *Human Nature* is a show about Smokey Robinson hits in the old Motown days. It was awesome. In fact, it is getting ready to go on tour around the country...look it up online. The other show was a tribute to the Bee Gees. Also a fantastic show. We also visited our old friends, Cheryl and girls, at the Keno booth and our friend Don in the sportsbook. Also visited with our favorite waitress at the Cafe every morning for breakfast...thanks Vera! Only ran into one asshole the whole Vegas trip, and I took her with a grain of salt—the kind of person who, if you were stuck on an elevator, you wouldn't choose her to be on it with you. You know...I had a better time trying to put on my underwear pregnant!

Anyway, trying to get well, and I'll be back with other little things that happened on our trip. What happens in Vegas stays in Vegas...I don't think so.

Hugs,

March 11, 2012

Okay...tomorrow is a big day. Please pray for good blood work results so I can have the last chemo tomorrow. Sure ready to have real hair again. Although, I'm not looking forward to taking the steroids once more...my butt is already the size of Dallas...but soon I'll be back in the pool and off the "fat formers." I'm not used to looking in the mirror and seeing a bald-headed hippo!

Please send a special prayer out to my pal Lindsay. While I'm having chemo tomorrow, she will be having a little procedure of her own. With the prayer network working for you...it will be a breeze!

Believe,

March 13, 2012

Good morning! Doing very well after chemo. THE LAST CHEMO...I might add. I think that's what makes it tolerable. Slept off and on last night with no nausea. Will probably do the same today. Craving everything in sight, as usual, thanks to the steroids! But no nausea. What can I say? I'm good. Chemo fog is slowly setting in. Have to reread everything I write several times. Always catching a few mishaps. If you find any, just bear with me. No reactions to any chemo drugs yesterday. Started the drip slow on the Taxol and then sped up. Carboplatin was okay too. Will probably get my usual rash today about 2 p.m. Never fails, and we still can't put a finger on what causes it, although several theories have been thrown out there. It really doesn't matter…you just have to live with it anyway. Thanks to my wonderful nurses, Betsy, Tracy, Susan, and Rena, for taking such good care of me. I love you all, but I hope I do not have to see you again for chemo reasons anytime soon. But I will see you tomorrow for the dreaded $8,000 white cell injection! UGH! Always makes my day!

Wanted to add something that happened at the end of our trip. When leaving Las Vegas, we got to the airport early to get a bit to eat before boarding, and of course, the wonderful "pat-down" I get at the airport. I think the port above my right boob throws the scanner off, so I just always get patted down. (A port is inserted for people to receive chemotherapy treatments without having to inject them intravenously each time.) Hey, probably better for me since I've been through so many medical scans in the last two years with cancer. Anyway, the winds were blowing 70 mph. The hotel limo was swaying all over the road. That was only the beginning. The plane was delayed because our connecting flight was not able to land due to all of the wind and a huge dust storm (you couldn't even see the buildings on the Vegas Strip), so it was rerouted to Ontario! Okay, our crew is in Ontario and now we are stuck until the airline can muster up a crew. We had two stewards and the airline was looking for one more. About an hour after we were supposed to take off, they gathered a pilot and co-pilot. I hated to ask from where...hopefully, it wasn't from a bar. Although that might have been a plus under these circumstances. Believe me, the Good Lord and I had a serious discussion...I've made it this far with the cancer curse...I ain't going down on this plane! Of course, plenty of Merlot helped...tremendously! We got seated and the steward was taking drink orders; I think it was a shrewd tactic to keep our minds off of the plane, parked at the gate moving back and forth to the rhythm of the wind. OMG, yes, two wines please... no wait, where is the winery? If Leilani has nine lives...I probably went through several! But we made it home and that's what counts. Lani, Casey, and my brother D took good care of Magoo.

Of course, Magoo had to have a problem right when I entered the door coming home from chemo. He has another toothache. I told Bill I am going to sedate him and pull his teeth out myself! Maybe I won't sedate him... hmmm. Don't mess with me in chemo fog! Not wise. Until we can get him a dentist appt. (spring break, dentist has kids and vacation), he is stuck with the oral gel treatments. Man, I shouldn't be in the clinical trials.... Dad should be.

Hope everyone has a great week. Check the blog often. I'm always adding stuff.

Ride, Baby, Ride!

March 18, 2012

Sorry for not writing. I have been a little under the weather. I'll try to catch everyone up on what's been happening. Had chemo Monday…was fine. Seemed to be fine all day Tuesday, and Wednesday morning, I had my $8,000 white cell shot. Went to pick up pills at the pharmacy and grab some Chinese for lunch. Started feeling a little nauseated Wednesday night. By Thursday, I was running 101 fever and throwing up. Friday morning, I felt pretty good. Well enough, I thought, to go out to the Houston Livestock Show and walk around and see the exhibits. Wrong! Almost passed out. Figured out that a bladder infection must have entered the picture somewhere along the line because I couldn't pee. Burned…hurt… but already on Augmentin, so I thought this should pass quickly. It did. But still coughing my head off and throwing up mucus. Sounds like a soap opera! But I feel I am in good company; half the people in Houston have the crud these days. Must be some mass biological attack by "our enemies" to make us all miserable.

Magoo is still complaining about his teeth. We will take care of that Tuesday. In the meantime, we are keeping Oral Gel in business. The man thinks it grows on trees. Anyone have Oral Gel seeds to plant? And if his Plavix goes up any higher in price, we'll all have to go out and try to find a job. Lani has the honors of dentist duty on Tuesday. I'm sure this ought to be good.

My sis-in-law Libby was house-sitting for the last month for our friends Linda and David. L&D went on a month's vacation cruise to "Down Under" and just returned. During this past week, Libby's mother fell and broke her leg. So please include Ellen's speedy recovery in your prayers. So, I'm glad of the return of our friends and anxious to visit soon. However, they both came back with the crud! Add two more victims to the crap! I'm sure my nephew Tanner (their dog) was so excited to have them back. Although our dogs love seeing Aunt Libby coming. She spoils them rotten!

I have heard from many of you whom Bill and I met on our trip. Thanks for your support with the book. It makes me feel so special that all of you are so supportive of the book and my determination to help the ovarian cancer cause. I will be sending info on a big fundraiser that we are undertaking to start an ovarian cancer research fund along with the proceeds from the book. Tell me if you have any fundraising ideas. I'm open to them all. Sounds like a big gathering in Fulshear and another in Houston.

Talk with you tomorrow with the Monday update.

Ride, Baby, Ride!

March 19, 2012

Good morning!

Yes, I said good. Seems like I'm just back down to the plain ole crud now. Chemo fog has lifted and nausea and bladder infection seem to have left the scene. Thank goodness! Seriously, I was sick! I don't complain too often, but all of that at once is too much for anyone.

To start off…no names mentioned to protect the guilty and the innocent…I have been told that someone had "a bone" to pick with me! So I listened and laughed my ass off. I have now decided that men need a special name for their privates. We cannot have little boys calling their genitals "who-has." So for all the men out there I will make sure that your "package" is called "rod and reel"! I would call it the "remote," but one might get confused since you always have that in your hands all the time too. I am flattered that the "who-ha" has become so popular, but I can see why men would not want their package called that. Problem solved!

I want to thank a friend of mine, Richard Phillips. He lives in North Carolina and his church sends me postcards monthly. I want you to know that I received one of these postcards right when I really needed it. I was sick and throwing up when Bill came in with the mail and said, "This ought to cheer you up." It made my whole day. The love that God sends is unending. Thanks, Richard.

You'll never know how much calmness that put in me. It was John 14:27: "Peace I leave with you; my peace I give you. I do not give to you as the world gives. Do not let your hearts be troubled and do not be afraid."

Tomorrow is Academy Award day again for Magoo. It's already started. Dragging his butt and moaning about his tooth. But when we leave, he sits down, watches TV, and I guess, thinks of his next move. He forgets we observe him 24/7 on the monitor. You really have to see it. When my sis-in-law Libby came by yesterday for a visit, did he ever bamboozle her. The rest of us sat in the house, watching and laughing. Anyway, Lani will have all the scoop tomorrow.

This will certainly be a week of catching up and trying to get things back in perspective. I'm supposed to have a PET scan sometime next week. Have not heard from St. Luke's on timing. I have a Dr. Bevers appt. on April 2nd, and I guess that should be it for a while. For all of you who have been through the cancer experience or know of someone who has experienced it, know that I am staying optimistic, but I am always looking out for my back. The time I spend with family and friends is so precious to me and not having to deal with the chemo every three weeks is definitely a plus. Please keep your prayers coming and know that I feel every one of them.

Pool dude, Scott, is here to make sure our pool is ready to go the minute I can possibly get in it. So have a great week and let me hear from all of you. Know that your love keeps me going. Something a friend sent me….A dog has so many friends because he wags his tail instead of his mouth. Sounds like a great life lesson to pay attention to.

Ride, Baby, Ride!

March 22, 2012

Okay…I didn't forget everyone was waiting for the Magoo episode with the dentist; I was just trying to figure out the best way to pass it on. Lani has been drinking ever since she got home. Mumbling words that sound like chants from the ancient Mayans. To start the "Tales from the Magoo Crypt," we will go back to 6 a.m. Tuesday morning. Bill and I are sound asleep when Dad yells into the intercom, "Is it time to get up?" I literally jumped four feet off the bed. (Of course, Bill didn't hear a thing…not that I expected him to). I told Dad to go back to sleep; it was only 6 a.m. At 6:15 a.m… ."Leilani, is it time to get up?" Okay…I've had enough. "Sure Dad…get up. I'll be over in two hours with your breakfast." At 6:30 a.m., the man is sitting in his chair dressed to go to the dentist. And that is where he was sitting when Bill served him breakfast at 8:30. We told him we would leave about 9:45 for his 10:30 appt. At 9:15, he was knocking on our door, ready to leave. Lani is just getting out of bed. He went ballistic. So he didn't talk to Lani the entire trip to the dentist, at the dentist, or back from the dentist. He spoke with all the girls there and to the doctor, but not to Lani. When we got back, he wouldn't talk to Bill and treated me like he didn't know who I was. Oh, well. That lasted for about ten minutes with me...until he needed something. Turns out there was actually nothing wrong with the teeth other than just being ninety-eight years old. Dr. Kaestner said he can only do so much, and then we might have to think about having a few of them pulled. Have not run that past Magoo yet. Probably won't until he starts complaining again. But now we are looking for a "shrink" for Lani. One who understands the Mayan dialect.

Good news. My CA-125 that was taken before the last chemo was a 2. So no change…thank goodness, and now just waiting on the PET scan next week. This time I'm going to insist that there is no pillow. My nose was way too close to the top of that machine last time. It really freaked me out. So pray for a quick and uneventful PET scan on the 29th—another fun day of being injected with the nuclear fluid and feeling like a ninja turtle. I just love glowing in the dark.

Had an e-mail from Dr. Mark Bing. So jealous…he is back on the train heading for Seattle. They had stopped at a beer garden somewhere and I was sent a pic. Wish I were there, Mark; it was so much fun. Also heard from several new friends whom we had met on our trip to Reno. Bill and I want to go out to California and stay at a winery/bed & breakfast and do some wine tours. Sounds like a vacation made in heaven to me! Any suggestions from any of y'all out there, please let us know.

Bluebonnets are everywhere. Front acreage looks just like the cover of my book. One of God's special gifts to us each morning I wake up during the spring. Couldn't ask for more. Mother mockingbird still comes every day to the front door for her daily handful of nuts. And the huge hawk is scoping out the bluebonnets for critters. And if there is a snake anywhere to be found…he'd better get it. Because if I see it first…people in China will wonder what that scream was.

Until next time…Ride, Baby, Ride!

March 27, 2012

One, two, three, JUMP! It was time to hit the pool yesterday. I was so ready for this. Got my fat, steroid ass in my swimsuit, grabbed my sunscreen, and my extra-large beach towel (just in case someone snuck up on me and I had to go incognito), and started my leg exercises and water weights. I have been waiting for the water temp to rise above 80 degrees, so yesterday we hit an 83. It felt so good. Anyway, I was enjoying the beautiful day yesterday, so I'm a little late on the Monday Update.

Everywhere I go, I'm on the lookout for snakes. Our neighbor Marvin informed us that he killed a big copperhead last week, and our neighbor behind us, who has all the cattle, said she shot three water moccasins that were sunning on a log in her pond. UGH! Lani and I got the shotgun out yesterday, too. Only it was for some guy thinking (or not thinking at all) that he was just going to come in our locked gate and walk up the driveway without causing a ruckus. Wrong! Once face-to-face with Moochie and Starr and with a bald-headed woman and her gun…he stopped dead in his tracks. Turns out he said he worked for Center Point and was changing out all the meters in the neighborhood. #1, he did not have a Center Point energy uniform on and was in an unmarked white truck. Just what did he expect two country girls to do? Nobody just makes himself at home out in the country where all the neighbors tote arms! Found out from others that similar incidents went on throughout the hood! I'm sure that after changing our meter, he had to change his underwear. I still can't believe a company that big would not call first or send a notice warning people that someone will be coming on a certain date. Big mistake on its part. Anyway, that will teach them to mess with Fulshear Farms. Hi-ho, Silver…away!

I will have a PET scan on Thursday. Oh, joy! So as soon as I hear something, I will let all know. I have an appointment with Dr. Bevers on April 2nd, so I should definitely find out something then. Other than that, I'm slowly getting over the crud. Not coughing as much, and I got off the Cipro so I could get in the sun. (Sun's a no-no with Cipro). Thanks for the e-mails, calls, and prayers. You all know how much I really appreciate the support and friendship. So, back to "reptile watch," and believe me, I will be packing my pistol as I roam "the back forty." As I have said since day one, the only good snake's a dead one! Better yet…not to encounter one at all! EEEK!

Hugs! Ride, Baby, Ride!

March 31, 2012

After fasting since midnight, I bravely entered the PET scan imaging center and took my place in line behind all the others dreading "the tube." Soon I was once again nuked with the radioactive crap and deposited in a room for forty-five minutes for the juice to flow through my system. I was very relieved to see my usual scan tech, Dawn, back from vacation. The last girl, if you remember, had my nose stuck to the ceiling or up my ass in that thing, so I almost lost it. Dawn had me as low as she could, and I only used a little bit of the pillow, so I wound up about five or six inches from the tube ceiling. Still awful, but tolerable. So I'm thinking of ways to pass twenty minutes. First of all, they play music in the room. So in my infinite wisdom, I figured out how to keep track of twenty minutes. I decided if each song was about three minutes long, it would take approximately seven songs to get me through. Needless to say, the first five went so slow. Next, I thought of things just to keep my mind busy while I was counting songs. How about PET scan tube graffiti? Have a Sharpie hanging in there and write stuff that everyone is probably thinking while stuck in this thing, like: "Leilani was here," "I can't breathe," "I've got to scratch my ass," "Where's the TV?", "Can anyone hear me?", "Beam me up, Scotty," "This end up," "I've got to pee," "Has anyone ever had sex in here?", and so on and so on. I would love to hear what you all would write. I'm sure the girls at PET imaging, Dawn and Leo, are going to kill me.

I have not heard from Dr. Bevers as to any results. He probably will not get them until Monday morning. So hopefully, he'll have them when I see him at 2 p.m. on Monday. I guess in this situation…no news is good news. But as soon as I know, I will pass it on. The Monday update will not be on the blog until I get back from the appointment…so check the blog late Monday afternoon. Special prayer network request while on the subject of Dr. Bevers….please send out a special prayer for another Dr. Bevers' patient who is needing our help….Please add Gwen to your prayer list. Thanks!

Have a blessed weekend on this Palm Sunday time of celebration. And let me hear from you. I will be a little nervous until I hear from the doctor, but I will try not to think too much about it. Easier said than done!

Ride, Baby, Ride!

Dogs, Horses, Snakes, Oh My!

April 2, 2012

Celebrate! PET scan negative on everything! From eyes to thighs. Dr. Bevers and I were both quite excited. Thank you to all who gave me strength to go on. Looks like the Good Lord has something laid out for me to do here in the near future. Probably just to keep bugging Dr. Bevers. So, nothing for three months and then another CA-125.

I did get to meet a lady and her husband today, whom I have been wanting to meet for a while now. So to Gwen…it was a pleasure, and next time you and hubby are in town, let's get together. Life is full of surprises and you are one of them. It is so nice to meet great people like you. By the way, owls are awesome! (Gwen collects owls.)

The only thing I need to add is there needs to be an antidote for steroids! I'm afraid to go to the zoo because the bull hippo might think I'm his cow. Although I have lost four pounds (thank goodness for swimming), that still doesn't make me feel any better. So…no trips to the zoo for a while until I shed another twenty! Whatever happened to the days where I was looking for my ass? Hell, now "it" makes a corner before I do!

My baby, Dusty, turns twenty-eight on Wednesday. So I will be celebrating all day Wednesday that I have three great kids and that I deserve a pat on the back. And I deserve every gray hair too…if I had hair!! All ass and no hair, go figure.

Keep in touch….Don't forget to check the blog at least three times a week. I still need you. It ain't over until the fat lady sings, and I ain't singing yet! Hugs from Fulshear.

Ride, Baby, Ride!

April 5, 2012

I will be in touch with my personal research program in the near future. Everyone has been asking about the details for the Leilani Essary Hurles Ovarian Research Fund. I am really excited about it, and I am determined to get the word out about this horrible cancer. Invitations are in the making for this incredible event. Stay tuned!

Remember the symptoms of ovarian cancer are: bloating, pelvic or abdominal pain, difficulty eating and getting full quickly, and the urgent or frequent need to urinate. Please see your doctor if any of these symptoms last more than a couple of weeks.

Ride, Baby, Ride!

April 9, 2012

Hope everyone had a wonderful and blessed Easter. The Hurles' house was alive with love and excitement. All the kids came and we enjoyed the Honey Baked Ham and brisket. Add to it the mac and cheese, green bean casserole, and all the extras, and we certainly could not complain, but counted our many blessings.

On Saturday, I had some errands to run, and when I returned home and was parking the Jeep, Bill was swinging two shovels around, telling me, "Quick. . .quick," which can only mean one of two things around here: He is either just about to kill Magoo, or there is a snake somewhere. I was really hoping it was the first one. Wrong! A three-foot water moccasin was right beside Magoo's walkway ramp. Lilly was having a fit. And of course, Dad, couldn't see it. Bill was screaming for him to get the dog inside and for him to stay in. Talk about a circus. Lilly had more sense than either one of them. So Bill has one shovel, and he gives me the one that kids play with on the beach to build sandcastles. "What the heck am I supposed to do with this?" I wondered, and I just know the snake was thinking the same thing... "Like she's going to chop at me with that!" By the time we finished, it was in several pieces. I kid you not. It looked like a sushi bar of snake parts.

God, I hate snakes. So, in my infinite wisdom, I had Bill find someone to cut down all the bluebonnets. I hated that because you know how I feel about my bluebonnets, but the weeds had grown so tall among them that I could just see snakes lurking in them and one of the dogs getting bit. So our wonderful neighbor Ernie volunteered for cutting duty. Bill and Ernie were out discussing their strategy. I called Ernie's wife, Bernie, to ask how they were communicating out there. Neither one of them could hear, especially over the lawnmower motors. It's the man thing...the torque crap…the penis talk code that only they understand. So as they were getting started, Ernie's mower breaks down. So off to Plan B. Our wonderful neighbor Marvin got a hold of his son-in-law Wade to bring his huge tractor over and wipe them out. Since Marvin is one of our local firemen, and he was on duty Easter weekend, he brought the fire truck over to watch the action. Neighbors were calling, thinking something was wrong. What could possibly be wrong at this house? OMG!

Good news though. The rhino rear-end is getting more muscular. And I am beginning to tan. That always makes you look thinner. And I am up to thirty laps a day. I can't tell you how much I am enjoying the pool. It gives me a whole new lease on life!

The horses had their vaccines this morning. Poco and Bud are so funny. It's like they know it's the vet when she drives up. We have to halter them before she gets here because they try to hide. But I made sure they got plenty of carrots and apples when she left. Spoiled brats! The dogs will have their turn on Thursday. Everybody hates the spring vaccines!

Have a great week everyone. Hugs from Fulshear!

Ride, Baby, Ride!

April 16, 2012

Last week was very busy. Got a lot done. And there are all kinds of things going on this week. Main thing… numero uno…was getting my teeth cleaned for the first time in a year. I was due for a cleaning last October, but I started chemo and could not get it done. There is no feeling like a good power-washing of the mouth. So thanks, Dr. Kaestner and the girls for making me feel sooooo much better.

I also had my port flushed out. All kinds of maintenance on this old body. It is always fun to visit and get hugs from the wonderful crew at Kirby Glen Infusion Center. My buddies, Betsy and Tracy, took good care of me. I will have to have the port flushed about every six weeks. I figure I'd rather have it cleaned out every six weeks than have it removed and have to have surgery again to put it back in if needed. And, hopefully, it WON'T be needed!

Bill and I had a week of spring cleaning. He did a lot of mowing and I did a lot of cleaning and rearranging. Got rid of many things we just didn't need or things that were just stacking up that other people said they wanted but never picked up. So we asked our friend John, who has a huge van, to come and haul a bunch of crap off to the dump. Feels almost as good as the teeth cleaning to rid ourselves of junk! At the end of that day, exhausted, we sat down to have a wine on the front porch. I sat in my rocker and Bill sat in his when I heard…"A SNAKE!" You know, the dreaded words that no one wants to hear or see. A rat snake was wrapped around Bill's wine holder. Our wine holders are iron and were bought at the rodeo a couple of years ago. They stand about 3' high, and there are horseshoes at the top where you place your wine glass. That horrible thing was about 4' long and wrapped all over the top of that holder. It was so disgusting. But he got away…he was really fast…which was even more disgusting. At least rat snakes aren't harmful. But I would much rather have him in a few pieces. Dr. Bevers sent me a picture of a snake killed at his ranch. It was a lot longer than ours. UGH! We have had several neighbors tell us about gator stories. Yes, alligators. So for Marvin's daughter and my friend Blis, who both live on the east side of Fulshear and close to rivers and creeks, be careful. Marvin's daughter couldn't get in her car to go to work because a gator was sunning next to her car. And Blis sent me a picture she took of a 7' gator that was in her yard. I think I'll stick to snakes and just carry my shovel around. On a good nature note, we have spotted woodpeckers in our front trees. They are beautiful and very curious.

This week I will be "journey bead" shopping for my friend Lindsay. Her twelfth birthday is Thursday, and I guess journey beads are the thing now. So I have seen several kits that she might like. If anyone has suggestions on journey beads, please let me know.

I was sent an e-mail that had a story about an ole guy being forced into moving to a rest home after his wife had passed away. He said every morning he makes the decision that it's not how things around you are arranged; it's how you arrange them in your mind. So every morning, free yourself from hate, free yourself from worry, live simply, give more, and expect less. Wow, what great advice. It seems to me a lot of this comes with age and we call it "wisdom." So yesterday, Bill and I snuck away for lunch with our good friends Linda and David. Dusty and Michele dad-sat, and he never knew we were gone. Lunch at Dekker's was awesome, and it was our way of freeing ourselves from worry.

Have a great week and stay out of trouble. Lots of events going on this week, so there will be lots of news next Monday. Hugs!

Ride, Baby, Ride!

April 23, 2012

Magoo is on the loose! And boy, did he have a special week. To begin with, he started complaining about his "Neanderthal" teeth again. But little did he know the gang was well ahead of him. Anticipating mouth trouble, the wonderful staff at Dr. Kaestner's office pre-scheduled an appointment…just in case! So the "teeth saints" went to work. By the way, the teeth saints include Dr. Kaestner, his nurse Carolina, and the incredible Gail who never lets me down when a "Magoo moment" arrives. God bless all of you. So Magoo's appointment was at 10:30 a.m.... Dad was on his front porch ready to go at 7 a.m. I s**t you not! The man was rocking in his rocker, fully dressed, and had his alarm clock in his hand. Even the mockingbirds were saying, "Do you know what time it is?" Anyway, we got his ninety-seven-year-old ass in the truck and threw his walker in the truck bed. (Probably should have switched those positions...what was I thinking?) Bill was in the back seat and removed his hearing aids for the ride into town. Dad kept talking to Bill and I kept telling him, "Bill can't hear you." Bill's butt was left at the corner of Chimney Rock and Richmond. Don't pick him up if you see him!

Friday night, I'm putting Magoo to bed, and he has taken everything off his nightstand and deposited the items on a chair on the other side of the bed. I'm totally confused as to what he is trying to tell me. Turns out, he said there was a lump in his bed and he needs a new mattress so he can get comfortable. Okay, my first thought is, "What is the lump in the bed? Did Lilly bring in another dead rabbit and hide it, or was it Lilly herself, or did Magoo leave something in the bed?" Could not find anything. Then he says he can't find his flashlight...it's not on the nightstand where it always is. Hello, nothing is on the nightstand...you moved everything...your flashlight is on the chair with all your other crap! It took a whole bottle of Merlot to get me through that night.

But besides driving everyone nuts, he was honored at a Big Brothers Big Sisters dinner where eight wonderful young people will get to go to college because of the Essary Scholarship Fund. My brother, Bill, Lani, and I got to meet the nicest families. Dad, unfortunately, could not attend because of his teeth pain. And thank you, Ron Hadley, President of BBBS, for all you have done to coordinate this wonderful event. The entire family is so proud.

My sidekick, Lani, flew off to South Carolina yesterday. Will be gone for about ten days. Stocking the shelves with plenty of "spirits." OMG…just Bill, Magoo, and moi! Lord, help me….I'm just waiting for one of them to "make my day." And you know what I mean! Other than that, I had a dermatologist appointment with Dr. Adam. You remember from the book that he is the doctor who used a magnifying glass on my "who-ha." Probably gave Dr. Bevers all kinds of ideas, as though he needed encouragement! This time, after a complete exam, I came away with only two small places to freeze. One on my right arm and one on my right cheek. Not that cheek… face cheek! Where are your minds? And my hair is slowly growing back. Head looks like a baby bird. All fuzz. And major announcement…ta-da…I had to shave my legs yesterday. Always a thrill….That's the one thing I liked about not having hair! Still Brazilian everywhere else. I knew all the men were waiting for that one to be answered.

Have a great week. Love you all!

Ride, Baby, Ride!

April 30, 2012

It's hard to pick which "man" to start with! So I'll just pick my wonderful, hard-of-hearing husband to talk about first. Bill was torn between sitting in his recliner, drinking a beer, and watching *Rambo* for the two hundredth time, or getting on the lawn tractor and tackling the dreaded horse field. With my wifely persuasion, I encouraged him to get off the recliner and put his bottom on the mower instead. So switching his beer to a bottled water, he set out to conquer a two-and-one-half-acre horse playground. Poop and all! He normally wears a ball cap and protective goggles, but it was late afternoon, so he decided, in all of his wisdom, to face nature free of gear. When he comes back in…bald spot on head sunburned, he says, "I think I got something in my eye." Okay, first of all…you *think* you have something in your eye? So as I play "Nurse Nancy," with Bill whining, the dogs start going berserk. Squirrel in the front alert! And lo and behold, Magoo decides to visit. What else can happen? You guessed it…the phone rings. And people wonder why I drink! So after I got everything settled and got back to Bill's eye, I noticed that it was extremely red in the corner. So I had him wash it out and, of course, put some Visine in there just to say I did something. Two days later at the eye doctor's office, I am watching as the doc takes Bill's eyelid, flips it up, takes a Q-tip, and goes to work. You'll never believe what was removed! Bug body parts! Only a piece of wing and leg…UGH. Dr. Goffman told me I need to learn the Boy Scout way of getting things out of the eye. I politely told him that I had never been a Boy Scout but a Girl Scout, and our deal was selling cookies. #1 Girl Scouts don't get things in their eyes, and #2 we are smart enough to wear goggles when mowing.

So now having to take Bill to the ophthalmologist, we were stuck with leaving Magoo home alone for a couple of hours. Remember, Lani will not be back from South Carolina until tomorrow night. Dusty and Casey were working and daughter-in-law Michele was without a car for the day. So instructions for Dad are "Do NOT go outside; you could fall off the porch. Make sure when you do get up, that you have your walker with you." I set out two bottled waters and a Dr. Pepper and made a sandwich for his lunch. Butter cookies for dessert. All set.

All goes well at the ophthalmologist. We return home and where is Magoo? He is on our back porch! Without his walker! With his sandwich in his hand! I'm sure you get the picture, except he only had on his pajama bottoms! No there is not enough wine in Napa Valley!

I have several great things to report. My friend Jenny, who lost her husband three years ago, has taken the big step to date again. I'm so proud of her. And to top it all off, she is going to be a grandma! Way to go, Jenny….I'm so proud of you. Life's too short; get out there and make the best of it! I also want to remind everyone that there will be a Cancer Walk at MD Anderson this Saturday. The info about the walk is on the blog that I posted a couple of weeks ago. Check it out. My pal Lindsay will be my reporter for the "walk happenings."

Still working on increasing my swimming laps. Now up to fifty each day. The water has been perfect, and there is no place I'd rather be than in the pool and working on decreasing the steroid weight. I feel like I have a "popcorn butt," and it exploded. Bill and I will be at the Astros game on Wednesday. My handsome Dr. Cook sent me tickets, and I am so excited to get away and relax. So everyone have a blessed week and enjoy the wonderful weather we are having.

Ride, Baby, Ride!

Magoo, Moms & Medicine

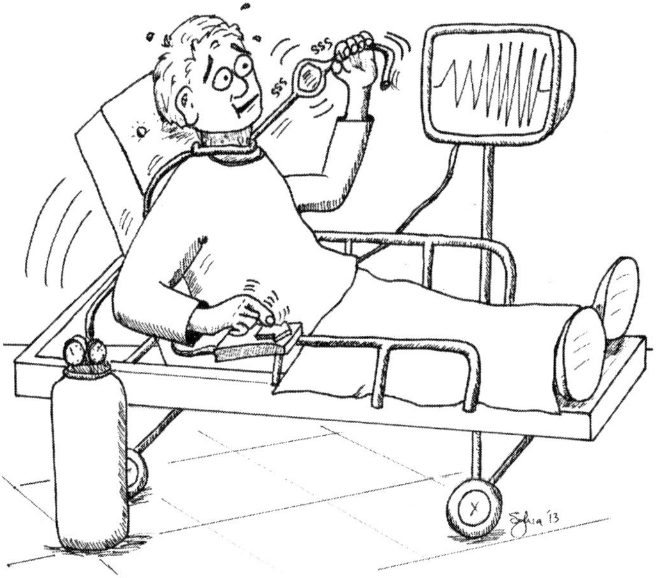

May 8, 2012

I have been asked questions about many things during my journey with ovarian cancer. I will share some of the questions I get and answer them. The most asked question is, "What was my reaction when I first found out that I had cancer?" Answer: Very mixed emotions. I know the first thought was…"I'm going to die! So how long do I have?" Then of course, "Why me?" Let it be known that cancer is not necessarily a death sentence. Scary… yes. But as time goes by, you learn that things are what they are. You have been thrown a curve ball and you deal with it. Don't feel sorry for yourself. Get out and find a way to play, just like everyone else. I believe the worst thing anyone can do is to give up on life. That's not part of the Man Upstairs' plan. I have been asked, "Did I feel bad before I was diagnosed?" Answer is...NO. The symptoms I had were so much like regular menopause stuff that I didn't pay any attention to them. The one thing I do know is that I had a feeling of a tiny pin poking at me from the inside down in the pelvic area. And a pain in my right shoulder and neck. And this is interesting because Dr. White (our family physician since I was a kid) told me that sometimes when something is wrong with the body, the pain appears somewhere else. And that many times, abdominal problems show up in the shoulder and neck area. At the time I was like…"What?" Boy, how true it was this time. Another question is "How do you keep your spirits up?" That is the hard part. I figure if you feel down and are always negative, you are going to sink yourself so low you will not be able to recover. I was lucky to have a very supportive team behind me. Family, friends, doctors, nurses, and my minister and his wife. I try to make it a point to meet new people every day. That is when you find that everyone you speak with either has or knows someone who has battled cancer. The many journeys people have taken are amazing. Not just with cancer but with all adversities. It has been a joy to meet so many new friends. You are part of God's plan and you will find out how you are part of it one day.

Bill, Lani, and I have been quite busy. My wonderful OB/GYN, Dr. Paul Cook, gave us Astros tickets so Bill and I got to go to the game. Great seats…right behind home plate. Lani had a dental appointment last Thursday, so we went on a lunch/shopping trip to go along with teeth cleaning. Saturday, Bill and I met our good friends Linda and David at the horse track and watched the Kentucky Derby. And yesterday, my handsome Dr. Bevers invited me to be part of a photo shoot with him to open the new MD Anderson Katy Regional Care Center. I met so many nice, caring people. So if you see my hippo butt and "the Bev" on a billboard around town...be sure and wave!

The rest of the week should be interesting. Magoo turns ninety-eight on Friday. He has been in rare form for the past week or so. He is really running out of steam. His friends are planning a little get-together at Dozier's BBQ on Friday. I just hope he makes it. It's no fun without Magoo antics…but we still have the hearing aid king to pick on! But every now and then, he revs up and moves pretty fast. Then we are all kinda like when you see the bomb tech go running by, you'd better try to keep up!

Tomorrow, Lani and I are driving to Cedar Creek, Texas (fifteen minutes from Bastrop) to have lunch with my swim team buddies, Jenifer and Cindi. I can't wait to see them.

Have a great week and stay out of trouble….I know; what fun is that? I can tell you all if friends were flowers, I'd pick all of you. Remember, your job is to keep me going. Hugs!

Ride, Baby, Ride!

May 10, 2012

I thought I would take this time to tell all that Lani's BRCA 2 lab results came back positive. She had a 50/50 chance of being negative. It is not good news in itself, but it does give us a heads up for her medical future. We will be working closely with Dr. Bevers and Dr. Cook to make sure we make the right decisions. Lani will have the CA-125 test twice a year (cancer marker for women), and she will be screened closely for breast and ovarian problems. We know if she decides to have children, all the parts will come out after the child-bearing duties! Removing the ta-tas is a choice she will have to make, like I will. It's like it really doesn't bother us, but the men in our lives are cringing at this moment. What is it with men and ta-tas? Keep Lani in your prayers. I will keep you informed. Until next time....

Ride, Baby, Ride!

May 13, 2012

Wishing all you moms out there a very Happy Mom's Day. I sure miss mine!

Ride, Momma, Ride!

May 15, 2012

First of all, the Monday update is late due to unforeseen circumstances. Bill was sent to the ER by our doctor Mark Bing yesterday afternoon. Bill has had chest pains and arm numbing since last Friday. But he did not say anything nor want to ruin my Mom's Day. Believe me... he didn't need a heart attack to kill him after I found that out. He is fine. Of course, there was a battery of tests and still more to go. A PET scan of the heart is coming up along with a stress test. The hospital stay was comedy in itself. Bill kept choking himself with his oxygen tubing, his hearing aids kept showing up in unbelievable places, his nurses had to repeat everything nine hundred times because he kept losing his hearing aids, and some poor man was making all kinds of unpleasant sounds in the room next door. One of Bill's nurses, Kathy, said when she was trying to keep Bill from strangling himself with the oxygen hose, she found something hanging from the part that sticks behind his ear. Guess? Anyway, at noon today, Dr. Odhav, his cardio dude, and Dr. Bing discharged him, to the ecstatic delight of the entire Memorial Hermann Katy Hospital nursing crew, I'm sure. You have never seen such a quick release. Bill keeps asking why it didn't take longer for him to get discharged. I do not have the heart to tell him. Of course, he wouldn't hear anyway. I would like to thank all the (Memorial Hermann) nurses in the ER, and on the 6th floor, the ER doctors, and of course, Dr. Mark Bing and Dr. Anil Odhav for all their devotion to Bill. He was truly blessed to have you all there.

Mom's Day was wonderful. All the kids, my brother, my nephew Walker, Bill, and Magoo all had planned a fully packed day. BBQ and football, pool volleyball, and a few brews were the menu for the day. Casey and Christina gave me a beautiful hibiscus plant, which the boys planted by the pool for me. Dusty manned the grill, and Magoo actually stayed awake the whole day. Of course, he has been a cocoon ever since. Must have worn out his little ninety-eight-year-old heinie.

Speaking of Magoo turning ninety-eight…we had a small birthday party for him on Friday at Dozier's BBQ. His "ninety-something" buddies, Dick Baile and Judge John Singleton, my brother, family friend Dennis, Lani, Bill, and I were all present for the event. The old friends sat together while the rest of us waited on them. It was great to see Dad having such a great time. We made it through without calling the EMS for anybody. No CPR was necessary, and we sat close to the restrooms…so there were no accidents! Why didn't I patent Depends!

I have to tell this story because it is just too cute. A couple of weeks ago when I picked up Lani at the airport, there was a family of ducks in the Park & Ride parking lot. They were walking along the fence line. Dad, Mom, and twelve ducklings. They were so amazing. When a person would walk by, the dad would run away from the rest of them...playing hurt. The mom would duck her head down (no pun intended) and walk by the fence like no one could see her. The babies kept so quiet. Then the dad would come back, and off they'd go together…just a quacking! I must have watched them for a good fifteen minutes. The love and protection they had for their family was so beautiful. There couldn't have been a more inspiring picture for Mom's Day or Dad's Day.

Love and hugs.

Ride, Baby, Ride!

May 21, 2012

Feeling good is such a plus. No doctors' appointments, no worrying about how the blood work is going to come out, don't care about your hair…or lack of it. LIFE IS JUST GOOD. It's almost like the calm before the storm, which I don't even want to think about. Have been keeping busy, and I wake up in the mornings really loving the opportunity to be alive and achieve a goal each day. Sometimes, my goals require a little mischief, but that's okay. My guardian angel flies pretty close to me and pulls me by the collar when I get a little too rowdy. Although my angel must have been well paired with me because it sometimes seems like we get in trouble together. Like the time…well never mind, this is a family blog!

Bill, Lani, TJ (Lani's boyfriend), and I all went to the wonderful gala given by the Big Brothers Big Sisters organization on Saturday evening. Met so many wonderful people and enjoyed seeing old friends. KPRC (Houston's Channel 2) had the emcee honors. Thank you, Owen Conflenti (morning anchor) and Mary Benton (news reporter) for sharing your talents for the gala. And of course, thank you to Jerome Martin, general manager and VP of KPRC Local 2, for your continued support. The "Big-Black-Tie-Ball Casablanca Style" was amazing. We all danced and auctioned and drank and gambled (fake, of course) throughout the evening. If you ever need a band, hire the Brent Van Sickle Orchestra. OMG! They played everything from Motown to Jazz. Our dinner table crew were Mark Boyle (KPRC news reporter), Mike (Bank of America), Charles, and my good friend and BBBS of Houston President, Ron Hadley. Great company.... Thanks for a fun-filled time.

Everyone in the horseracing world is all excited now. "I'll Have Another" is now one race from winning the triple crown. So, Belmont is in three weeks....We will soon know. Bill went to the track to place our bets before getting dressed for the gala. All favorites came in, so the payoffs were minimal. Okay...ready for a Bill story? He gets back from the track and changes into his tux. We are on our way to the Houstonian Hotel and all seems normal. Well, as normal as it gets with Bill. Anyway, throughout the night, I'm asking him if he is okay because he is on new meds due to his chest pains last week. All seemed fine till we hit the dance floor. No, not literally; he didn't fall, but it was close. I noticed he was acting differently. As we were getting ready to leave, he couldn't find the valet ticket for the Jeep. Then while we were all looking through our pockets and purses, Bill disappears. Now... where is Bill? We look over on the park bench in front of the hotel walkway, and there is Bill sitting next to and talking to the statue of some dude with boots on, and people are taking pictures of him. Then Lani joins in by sitting in the statue's lap, just making it more fun for the passersby. An HPD (Houston Police Department) officer is sitting on the wall watching everything, and what does Lani do? She goes over and sits with the officer and just starts carrying on a complete conversation about everything. This guy is probably saying, "These people are actually getting on the road to drive home." Not to mention, the cop pointed out, that TJ's car's inspection sticker was expired. It was a hoot! Sunday morning… first thing…Bill is looking for his hearing aid. I told him it was making so much noise (loud beeping sounds) that I threw it out of the Jeep window! Are you ready for this? He said, "Where about on the freeway?" Funeral services are pending!

I have a speaking event coming up. A local book club has invited me to speak about *Ride, Baby, Ride!* and I will have more details later. Please know, if anyone would like to have a group event and would like for me to speak about the ovarian cancer experience and the book…just e-mail or call me. Getting the word out about ovarian cancer is the goal. Other than that, we are waiting for Bill's stress test and heart PET scan, which is scheduled for this Thursday. Prayers needed for Bill…in more ways than one!

Hugs, and Ride, Baby, Ride!

May 28, 2012

Happy Memorial Day to all. Honoring our heroes past and present is the agenda today. Thank you to all our fighting men and women who keep our country safe every day. To my dad who served in World War II as a reconnaissance pilot in the U.S. Army and to my hubby Bill who served in the U.S. Air Force during the Viet Nam War, I am so proud of you. And a special thanks to those who made the ultimate sacrifice. God did bless the USA!

A quick summary of Bill's testing that was done on Thursday. We have not received any results back. It's always bad to have any type of testing done right before a holiday. I think the whole medical industry takes off a day before the holiday weekend starts and slowly filters back in after it's over. So we probably won't hear anything until Tuesday. The test went well. Bill was very dizzy and nauseated afterwards. They did the stress test along with the heart MRI. Not quite sure how that works, but it should spit out the results the doctor is looking for. So, hopefully, Bill's cardiologist, Dr. Odhav, will have good news for us.

As for me…doing nothing except swimming, catching up on my Nora Roberts novels, and watching my hair grow. Watching my hair grow everywhere! Brazilian look is out. I'm now going with the "hairy beast" look. It's so hard during that transitional period. Everything itches! It's not very "lady-like" to go around scratching the crotch. Shaving the legs, plucking the eyebrows, waxing the lip, and getting to put mascara on the eyelashes have all been missed little pleasures of life, but they are now back. I'm loving it. It actually takes me more than three minutes to shower now. Washing my hair is great, and it only takes a minute to dry. See…it doesn't take much to amuse me. My son Casey (middle kid) shaved my neckline for me Saturday, which felt really good. First haircut in almost eight months.

Bill and Magoo have been good boys. Any time war movies are on 24/7, I get relief. Give the two of them (in separate houses, of course, so they don't fight) a remote and snacks and a cooler of drinks to sit next to their recliners and I have the makings of a peaceful, non-interrupted, Nora Roberts, floating in the pool with a glass of wine fest! I might even get a nice tan out of this. It has been too hot for Magoo to come out anyway. I threatened him with his life the other day when he almost fell while trying to get out of his porch swing. "Dad," I told him, "it's too hot; stay inside till this evening when it cools down with a nice breeze." In one ear and out the other. At least it goes in with him. Bill just sits there where my voice tries to go in one ear and meets a barricade. Oh well!

I will be adding a few blogs this week…when we get Bill's results back and a couple of announcements. Have a great Memorial Day. GOD BLESS AMERICA AND OUR WONDERFUL TROOPS!

Hugs!

Ride, Baby, Ride!

May 29, 2012

Unfortunately, I do not have good news about Bill. Dr. Odhav called us last night and said that the two tests given to Bill showed something wrong with his heart. MRI showed some blockage and the stress test was not good...or something along that line. We will be meeting with Dr. Odhav to go over the test results and decide on when to do an angioplasty. Bill has been taking his meds as directed and has only had one episode of chest pain since his hospital stay.

I will keep you informed on his progress. Please continue to pray for healthy results.

Ride, Bill, Ride!

Magoo & Bill Strike Again!

June 1, 2012

Okay...news from Bill's doctor and news from mine.

Bill will be having an angiogram on Tuesday morning. If anything is found, the doctors will take care of stents and balloons at that time. Dr. Odhav showed us the pictures of the MRI and stress test, and we feel certain there is some blockage. Not sure how much. But we will see.

As for me…CA-125 was a 3.8. Last one was a 2. I'm hoping that the difference is in the calibration of different labs. Dr. Bevers is such a sweetheart, and he is trying to keep me calm because he knows that I really get panicky about my CA-125. We will take another test in two months.

So please keep both of us in your prayers. More in my Monday update. "Life is a banquet and most poor suckers are starving to death." (From the movie *Auntie Mame* with Rosalind Russell)

Ride, Baby, Ride!

June 4, 2012

Have to begin with a Magoo story. My daughter-in-law Michele turned me on to a new app on my cell phone. She knows how involved I am with *Ghost Adventures* (aired on the Travel Channel). So she found a Ghost Radar app. I have had so much fun with it. While testing it out, Bill and I went out on the patio to sip our wine and indulge the spirits (the ghost ones that is). The first thing the spirits said was "porch." Then "shade," then "author," then "airplane." Airplane—just as a jet was going over our house. Okay, not creepy enough for you. It said "burro." Bill and I looked at each other and said, "Since Magoo's not outside, which ass is it referring to?" (LOL) Just about that time, this donkey in the next field let out this horrendous noise. The neighbors had acquired a donkey. It gets better. I'm putting Dad to bed and the spirits were talking as I was showing him my new app. The next morning, Bill goes to feed Magoo breakfast, and Magoo tells him not to leave that machine over here at night anymore. The ghosts talked to him all night! Folks…I had my phone with me all night on my nightstand. We still have not figured out that one. Either Magoo has finally lost it or the ghosts had a field day messing with him all night. I really hope it's the latter.

Our grandson Braden came over to help Bill mow and do outdoor chores. Son Dusty and daughter-in-law Michele were here, too. Bill, Dusty, and Braden were trying to get a 100 ft. outdoor electric cord untangled. OMG, talk about entertainment. Michele and I were watching from the window. The Three Stooges at their best. It got to the point where we almost felt sorry for them…I did say almost!

The real donkey is a jenny (a female). Therefore, we do not consider her a jackass. Bill asked Lani and me why she wasn't considered a jackass, too? We rest our case! Should have sent the Three Stooges over there to ask her for help with the extension cord.

Momma cardinal is still sitting on her nest in the hanging bicycles. We should be grandparents again real soon. We also rescued a huge water turtle from the horse field. Bud and Poco (our horses) didn't seem to mind him. But we took him down to Bessie's Creek so he could be back home. The mockingbirds, hummingbirds, and wrens all seem to be keeping busy and eating us out of house and home. Don't believe the phrase "eats like a bird." If someone tells you that and you are supposed to be taking the person to dinner, hide your credit card!

Bill is getting geared up for his angiogram tomorrow. We have to be at the hospital at 6 a.m. It is referred to as "outpatient," but if more needs to be done, then he will have to stay overnight. I will update you ASAP after the procedure. Lani and I are going to the "dress rehearsal" tonight of the musical *The Best Little Whorehouse in Texas.*" Our friend Natalie Young works for Theater Under the Stars (TUTS) and was so nice to get us tickets for the event. So I will have a very short night. Probably won't get in until midnight, and then I'll be up by five to get to the hospital. A woman's work is never done! So prayers for Bill please.

Thanks to Linda and David, our good friends, for meeting us for lunch and helping to take our minds off of everything else. Thank you to Dr. Bevers and Bles for making me feel so special when they are truly the special ones. They have moved into the new MD Anderson facility in Katy. It's beautiful, I might add. I got a kick out of the new examining tables. Like I told my friend Gwen (who is also a Dr. Bevers' patient), "It's like going up in an elevator…naked!" I don't think I've ever been that high up with my legs spread! Not even in my college days. Unless you count the chandelier party…oh well, that's a different story. And for my minister, my hero in the black robe, Dave Peterson, just try not to think about what I just said. Your job to get me through the "pearly gates" is hard enough.

Remember, when you look in the mirror, see yourself doing great things. Don't give up. Positive all the way! Hugs!

Ride, Baby, Ride!

(Note: My friend Gwen passed away the following September to ovarian cancer)

June 10, 2012

Hi Everyone,

Bill is home after sailing through his triple bypass. The doctor would not allow visitors in the ICU or his suite. It made for a quick recovery. Bill is an amazing and strong man. He will have to take it easy for about six weeks. The doc says no tractor riding for a while, which has him in a tailspin! Our neighbor Ernie is out mowing for him now, and Bill is drooling at the mouth with envy. I posted a note on Facebook and I will have a full update here tomorrow. So many funny things happened at the hospital. And much to tell about the amazing staff. I made so many new friends and such caring ones at that. Much needed sleep and rest is in the forecast. Give us about six weeks to get right and we will have a party to celebrate life. Love you all. Cowgirls only cry when their cowboys are having triple bypasses.

Ride, Baby, Ride! Hugs!

June 11, 2012

My husband is the most incredible man in the world. I will repeat some of the basic stuff for everyone. I sent a shout out yesterday on the blog and on Facebook to let everyone know we were home from the hospital and that Bill is doing fantastic. Could not have asked more from my cowboy. After the angiogram on Tuesday, it is mostly a blur. Dr. Odhav, Bill's cardio guru, sent for Dr. Olsson, a heart surgeon, to talk to us. We could not have been more pleased with our team. We, as a team, decided that the surgery was urgent enough to be done ASAP. So we agreed on the next morning. After much hoopla, we got everything arranged and set up for the next morning

(Wed.). At 7:30 a.m. Bill was wheeled into surgery for either a triple or quad bypass. (Turned out to be triple, thanks to some wizardry by the doctor). Dr. Olsson performed the five-and-a-half hour surgery. Head nurse Marcia came out every hour to inform me about what was going on. Around 1:30 p.m., Dr. Olsson came out to let me know that Bill had sailed through the procedure with no problems. He did not need any blood, and he would be out of recovery and in ICU in a few hours. Lani met Dr. Olsson while bringing me something to eat and she had the okay to go with me to ICU to see Bill. No one else was allowed in. Let me tell you, the first look at your loved one with that respiratory tube shoved down his throat is not pretty. But he was breathing on his own, so he got rid of that quickly. Did I say I had the most incredible husband? The doctors could not believe how well and how fast he was recovering. On the second day in ICU, Dr. Olsson said he was already a day ahead of schedule. Each day proved to be more remarkable than the preceding one. He walked 200 feet the second day. I was floored. So we are now experts in several facets of medicine. Man, I thought cancer was a real trip....This, my friends, is nuts!

Anyway, we got home. We thank God every day for our wonderful doctors, nurses, and hospital staff, who have never ceased to amaze us with their kindness and efficiency. And thank you to our friends and family who were so understanding in not bugging us during this time. We asked for our time together and you gave it to us. Thank you to Lani and sis-in-law Libby for Magoo-sitting. Those two took care of Dad, dogs, horses, mail, papers, housecleaning, and all that goes with a hospital stay. And last but not least, to neighbors Ernie and Bernie for being nice enough to mow our property for us.

There were several memorable moments. The ICU ward does at times sound like the maternity ward. The sounds of moans and groans are creepy—Bill's included. Lani, the ICU nurse, and I were laughing so hard while poor Bill was in La-La Land. The noises that came out of that man were indescribable. We had a match for every sound we heard! Then there's the great little hospital gowns. After the tenth time I had to pull Bill's out of his butt crack, I decided I needed to invent a new hospital gown. Sometimes it's hard to tell what's imaginary and what is real. I was walking to the gift shop to get a few things, and as I approached the elevators on the sixth floor, the fire alarm went off. All the security doors shut. Announcements said not to use the elevators but the stairs. Hello….you shut the doors…there are no stairs. I freaked out. Waving with a Kleenex through the huge glass windows down to the security desk to let them know I was stuck, what do I see? The guard drinking a Coke and looking at his monitor. Must have been a big fire…right? Anyway, turns out it was a fire drill. I plan on calling the hospital about their techniques for performing a drill. Some old person would have had a stroke! I used to think that my idea of camping was black and white TV or staying at the Holiday Inn. Just changed my mind—it's a hospital stay. Ugh!

I feel like a big rock in a stream. Water keeps rushing by. It slaps away at your inner self. Sometimes, it rushes by, slapping you harder and harder. Other times, it ripples by, very slowly, feeling so good. But the water is there, no matter what. As long as the creek doesn't dry up, I feel secure. Such is life.

I will be putting progress reports on the blog this week to let you know how Bill is doing. I have cancelled my speaking engagement for tomorrow night. But I will make it up to the book club that I was supposed to speak to. As much as I hated to cancel, not only can Bill not be left alone, but neither can Dad. Lani and I are running double duty. We are doing what has to be done with Dad, all of Bill's chores, plus our normal stuff. But we have a system and all is going well.

So keep the prayers coming. I have my monthly port cleaning on Thursday. But other than that, no plans. Our anniversary is June 20th. We had planned to go to Vegas. That is now on the back burner for a few months.

Hugs! Ride, Baby, Ride!

June 14, 2012

If it is a six-week recovery, we just nailed one! Five to go. Bill has been doing great. He has discomfort (not pain), but mostly, it is from not being able to get comfortable enough to rest well. The incision looks good and the shortness of breath comes and goes, which is also normal at this time. He takes pain pills every 4-6 hours, depending on how his day is going. Stool softeners are helping with the pooping end of it. All I can tell you is that men are worse than children when it comes to not feeling well…and so demanding. So unlike Bill normally. But perfectly understandable. Bill has two doctors' appointments tomorrow. His cardio guy in the morning and his surgeon in the afternoon. We have written down a few questions for them.

I had my port cleaned out today by Tracy at St. Luke's Fusion Center. Always good to see and talk with my girls. Betsy still isn't back from her knee surgery. So I missed not seeing her. Hopefully, she will be back in the saddle again real soon. I'm enjoying this cancer free time, and I hope it stays away for a long time. I am totally devoted to Bill's recovery and so glad the Good Lord didn't let them both happen at the same time.

Hugs. Ride, Baby, Ride!

June 15, 2012

Awesome day. Great news. Doctors can't believe the progress Bill is making. I make him walk twice a day to our main gate and back. The incision looks like he might have just cut himself. And both doctors said Bill just came in to brag that a seventy-one year old can outdo their fifty-year olds. We are both having a glass of wine as I type. Both doctors agreed on that too! Got to love modern medicine!

Ride, Baby, Ride!

June 18, 2012

Hi, Everyone,

Hope you had a fun and safe Father's Day weekend. I have decided that I am just going to go ahead and commit myself to the mental institution so no one else has to bother. Gee, I think I've said that before, but this time, I mean it! Magoo pulled one of his greatest performances ever. Bill has been getting way too much attention. So Dad practically crawls (and I mean a "one breath from leaving this world and bothering the angels" crawl) over to our house and says his teeth are loose. Not just one but two. Sis-in-law Libby and I did a tooth inspection and found no loose teeth. He would not let up the entire weekend. So, I called Dr. Kaestner's office and talked to my friend Gail to see whether she could save the entire family from another performance from Magoo. Dad has an appointment tomorrow at 2 p.m. Lani will be his chauffeur for the day. I'll have the wine chilled when she returns! The staff at Dr. Kaestner's office is on their own.

But I have outsmarted "the Magoo." His dog Lilly is due for her shots. So while Lani is depositing Dad's butt at the dentist, I made an appointment for Lilly to get her shots at the same time. That way, he won't make a big scene at the vet's office. That is always an Academy Award in itself!

Bill is doing great. Gets stronger every day. Doctors' appointments went very well, and we are definitely on the right road to recovery. The doctor told him to eat whatever he wants (even hamburgers) to get his strength back up. Then it will be a heart healthy diet. But he is allowed to drink his red wine each day. That makes for a very happy Bill and a very happy Leilani and Lani. He's almost back to normal when he has that wine goblet in his hand, and is not throwing orders around right and left. Son Dusty and grandson Braden came over Saturday and Sunday to mow and trim trees, etc. Big help! Our neighbors Ernie and Marvin have been taking charge to make sure the acreage stays beautiful. Thank you both so much. Lani and I are handling the Bill chores pretty well. I took all the trash out this morning. (I can't wait till he can do that again.) So coffee in hand, wearing nightshirt and house-shoes, I drove the golf cart to the road and deposited all the trash for the garbage dudes to pick up. Then I couldn't find the gate remote. OMG…I hope I didn't pack it with the trash! So I had to do a scavenger hunt to find it. It was on the floor of the cart under the last bag of trash. I didn't know that I knew that many cuss words. I think I even made some up!

Got to float and read in the pool yesterday for a while. The sky was so beautiful. Did my laps doing the backstroke so I could observe all the beauty. Saw the American flag flying in the breeze, airplanes, butterflies, dragonflies, wasps, limbs swaying on the oak tree near the pool, birds of all kinds (just hoping the ducks didn't decide to poop on me on their fly over), and all the clouds. The beautiful clouds…all shapes and sizes. So much fun deciding what they remind you of. God is truly amazing!

I posted a picture on Facebook that was taken at the MD Anderson photo shoot. Still not sure when the photos will hit the billboards around town. There were several really good ones of Dr. Bevers and me. There are also some book dates coming up. A couple of them will be combined with a jewelry show. Proceeds of the books will go to my Leilani Essary Hurles Ovarian Cancer Fund. The lady who makes the jewelry has been kind enough to donate some of her earnings from the jewelry as well. Again, thanks for the cards, e-mails, calls, and visits. Bill enjoys them all. Hugs!

Ride, Baby, Ride!

June 25, 2012

I would like to start this blog with a special announcement. On Saturday The Leilani Essary Hurles (Bevers/Cook) Ovarian Cancer Research Fund officially got started. A dear friend of mine, Tajana, had a jewelry show, featuring her mother's beautiful handmade jewelry. In addition, she featured me as a guest speaker and gave a portion of her profits to our Ovarian Cancer Fund. It was at the beautiful ranch home of Josephine A., and many wonderful people attended. I enjoyed meeting all of you. Thank you to all who donated to the fund and to all of you who bought books. It was my pleasure to sign them for you. There will be fundraisers in the future, and I will keep you informed on dates and times. The next official event is July 21st here in Fulshear. Details will be announced soon. In the meantime, if you know of others who would like to give to the fund, please let them know that they can mail checks or money orders to:

Leilani Essary Hurles Ovarian Cancer Research Fund
PO Box 985
Fulshear, TX 77441

We need to get the word out about the "silent killer." I know that my part is small, but I'm trying, and many women's lives depend on it. I will send a receipt for all donations to the donors. I am putting in $5,000 of my money, and with the start we got on Saturday…we are on our way! MD Anderson is an amazing place, and I am happy to raise money in my name for it.

The next storm in the Gulf of Mexico should be named Magoo! He had no trouble throwing one of his wild curve balls on Saturday. You talk about spinning and going nowhere! Dad decided that when I left for the fundraiser,

I should be back by 5 p.m. Don't ask me how he does his math....I don't want to know or even try to figure it out. Bill said Dad paced his porch and our porch for an hour, waiting for Lani and me to get home. So afraid I was going to miss *Wheel of Fortune* with him. When we got home, I went over and I got the silent treatment. I explained about making money for the fund and selling books. Magoo put his hands over his ears and shook his head. He did not want to hear anything. I just got up and left. I think he finally talked to us last night. Out of necessity, of course...he needed a dose of milk of magnesia. If Magoo can't poop, we are all in for a bad day!

My friend Gail, the guru at Dr. Kaestner's office, sent me an e-mail of a wine cellar that was built into the floor of a home's kitchen. It was awesome. It had see-thru Plexiglas doors that opened, and you stepped down into a spiral staircase, and as you took each step further into the abyss, the walls were filled with wines. A wine/storm cellar all in one! Now that's my place to be in case of a disaster! I'd probably be yelling, "Tornado coming!" all the time. No flies on my ass!

Bill is getting better each day. We are taking walks several times a day and working on the little things that everyone else takes for granted. He is supposed to start rehab this week at the hospital. The physical therapist has exercises to teach us to do at home. OMG...where is that wine cellar? This ought to be a hoot. Men are such babies, and

Bill is no exception. I'm just about ready to pitch him a tent on the back forty! To all our wonderful neighbors who have helped so much during this ordeal, please check on this old broad. Once rehab starts, I'll either be hanging from the rafters with a Merlot in tow or Bill will show up missing!

The weather here in Houston has been so hot. Supposed to have several days in a row over 100. I think they said 104 or 105 today. Add that with the humidity and it is time to head for the pool and stay in there. Skin looks like a prune, but you're cool. We are fortunate to have bubblers in our pool, which adds a little extra coolness to the water. Not to mention the very soothing sound that relaxes you. I know I was born under the Aquarian sign for a reason. I have always loved the water, and I pray that the world can share the peace I get from the tranquil rippling sound.

Don't forget to get the word out about the fund. Let's blow this ovarian cancer crap out of the water! Any donation will help. Love, hugs, and prayers to you all.

Ride, Baby, Ride!

June 28, 2012

Life Without Lani

July 2, 2012

REHAB means…Rent out…Exasperating…Husband…After…Bypass! Between dealing with Magoo popping in about five times a day to check on Bill and Bill snapping at everyone for no reason, I am prompted to rent them both out….No, sell them! Magoo has made it his mission to torment Bill by walking in and waking him up. Actually, he is tormenting me because Bill goes right back to sleep and I have the duty of running him off. It's hard to explain Bill's problem. I know the feeling of being creeped out by pain and of having the bejesus scared out of you by going through a life-threatening event, but he needs to let up a little. He quips and is sharp with people. I'm sure it will pass, but it is enough to drive me crazy.

Lani left yesterday to visit "Mr. Wonderful" (love you Timothy) in South Carolina. I always track her with the "Flight Tracker" website. I was freaking out when I saw her plane going all over the eastern seaboard! She was supposed to land in Columbia, SC but managed to circle it twice and then they headed south to Charleston. They were diverted there due to the bad storms going through that region. She was supposed to land in Columbia at 5:13 p.m. EST but finally landed there at 9 p.m. EST. Lani said she sat next to a traveling pilot, and he kept showing her on his electronic device that they were not where they were supposed to be. Lani mentioned there wasn't enough beer on the plane! Not to mention that the pilot of the United Express Jet looked like he was nineteen. After refueling in Charleston and getting more adult beverages on board, the teenage pilot got my child to Columbia.

Got up this morning to get the trash out, and in the middle of the pool was the cutest water frog. This frog was positioned at the bottom of the pool on its hind legs, ready to leap at the next bug that swam by. Kung Fu Frog! Seriously, he had his little hands up in the air and his legs in squat position. I haven't had to remove any bugs from either of the skimmers or the top of the water in weeks. He does as much as "Cooter Brown" (what we named our pool cleaner) does, and you don't have to replace any parts. All he needs is a little bandanna!

My childhood friend Patrice called me last week to inform me that her sister Judy was going to be in town and wanted to try to get together for a visit. It's kinda hard for me with Bill and Magoo, but we managed a few hours together to talk over old times. It was so good to see them both. Time flies and we go way too far between visits. Son Dusty and grandson Braden came over and helped with all the mowing. I made my list of To-Dos. Everything from feeding dogs and horses, taking out trash, taking the pool sample, cleaning all the houses, laundry, grocery list, bathing dogs, cooking enough so I don't have to do it every day, and setting up and getting everyone to doctors' appointments. Oh well…makes the days go fast. Lani will be gone ten days. It's only been one and it seems like five.

Bill is supposed to start rehab this week (the real one). Have not heard from the hospital on his schedule, but I should hear something soon. Dr. Odhav's nurse has been working on it. I am due for another CA-125 test this month and probably an exam too. I will get with Dr. Bevers on our timing. It's time to give the who-ha some attention!

Thank you, Tony (Tone Dog Media) for helping me iron out a few things on my website. I am trying to get a fan page started for Facebook. I will get back to everyone on that. And thanks to friend/writer/editor Melanie Saxton for the wonderful article that you wrote about *Ride, Baby, Ride!* in the *Katy Christian Magazine*. If anyone is interested, my story is on page 30 of the June/July issue. It can be found at CVS Pharmacies and H-E-B'S (and many more places) in the Katy area. AND IT'S FREE! There is also a story about a friend of mine who owns a pet business called "Privileged Pets." Fiona and hubby Jack have a boarding kennel and pet-sitting service. Jack also trains dogs. If you need more info, visit their website (**www.privilegedpets.com**). They are a wonderful couple and your pets will be glad you did. More to come out too about the fundraiser on the 21st of this month. Have a wonderful week, my friends. Hugs to you all.

Ride, Baby, Ride!

July 5, 2012

July 9, 2012

OMG! You never know how valuable something is until it's missing. As I try to make it a few more days without losing my sanity, I realize how easy it is actually to "go off the deep end," "kick the bucket…and miss," to have your "elevator miss a floor," your "deck missing a card," your "nut missing a bolt," or have "a screw loose"! And I have one main cause for it all. MAGOO! Bill is manageable… Magoo is so out-of-control. The man has to hog all the attention. He goes to every length to drive me and Bill up the wall. You would think a ninety-eight-year-old man would sleep 98 percent of the day. No, I have to inherit the Energizer Bunny! The bunny equipped with a walker and house shoes that never wear out. The Superman of senior citizens makes at least five trips a day over here, in the heat or drizzling rain, to antagonize me. Bill sleeps through most of it, either because he doesn't hear him (go figure) or his pain pills are doing their job. I thought about taking a few of those with a glass of wine, but I decided that I'm crazy enough without all the hoopla. Lani is due back tomorrow, but she is thinking about staying a few extra days. I hope she is having a blast…because her mom…is NOT! Lani, you are missed and I love you.

You can always tell how much fun you've had by looking at your American Express bill. What I need to buy is a servant. A "taking out trash" servant. A "looks like George Strait" servant. I have lost four pounds just doing the Bill thing. Not to mention breaking nails and opening and closing horse gates. Okay…enough bitching about it. I am on a mission now. I work part of the day, then relax, get online, and buy stuff! I'm getting really good at it. Not like cruising the mall, but when you are confined to the casa…make the best of it. Just got the Am Ex bill in….I've had a ball!

Someone once wrote, "A true friend is someone who thinks you are a good egg even though they know you are slightly cracked." Well…I know I'm slightly cracked, but I also know I have many friends, and I am very grateful. This past week, I learned of another friend who will lose her fight with ovarian cancer after fighting for only a short while. I will not mention names, but I feel that my need to get my research fund moving along is more urgent than ever. Fighting for your life has become a daily thing for many people. Please pass the word about ovarian cancer and our fight to win. Any amount will be greatly appreciated. More info will be given on the address, etc. Or just mail your donation to:

Leilani Essary Hurles Ovarian Cancer Research Fund
PO BOX 985
Fulshear, TX 77441

Love you all,

Ride, Baby, Ride!

July 16, 2012

"These are the times that try men's souls"...Thomas Paine wrote in his 1780 series of pamphlets *The American Crisis*, inspired by his passion for the American Revolution. Ole Tom only had to worry and deal with a revolution...I have MAGOO! These are the times that try Leilani's soul. I have officially been mooned by Magoo. Believe me, the bare-bottomed sight of your father's ninety-eight-year-old ass is not the most appealing scenery I can think of. He was having a bout with constipation. Dad never wears a Depends except...when I double-dose him with milk of magnesia to shut him up. He doesn't let up when he can't poop. It drives everyone crazy. I went over to check on him, and he dropped his pants and said, "Do I have these on correctly?" OMG! They would have fit better if he had put them over his head! So he bends over right in my face to sit on the bed. I do not need to describe this sight. You may not eat for a week. I didn't! I am now the officer in charge of the proper way to install Depends.

Bill, on the other hand, has been a pretty good boy. Getting stronger each day, but he still sleeps quite a bit. But when he is up…I want to shoot him! He not only piddles…he roams the house and piddles. Not only does he roam the house and piddle…he roams the house and piddles right where I need to be. If I'm in the kitchen, trying to cook or cleanup, there he is. Right in my space where I can't move. Usually with his back to me, just staring out into space. "Earth to Bill! Move your butt!" "Oh," he'll say, "I didn't know you were there…." HUH?

Also disturbing is that in the middle of one of the huge thunderstorms we have had lately here in Houston...our pool pump blew up! Literally. I heard it and ran outside to where the pool equipment is and the damn thing was smoking! So I went and poured me a wine and watched it send smoke signals while I called the pool dude. I really think the rain helped it not catch on fire. Should be fixed today...hopefully. That's one problem I don't need added to my plate. The pool is my refuge, and it has to be available at a moment's notice. Ahhh!

Lani flies in tonight. Celebration! I have truly missed her more than she will ever know, but she so deserves the vacation. She said she had a wonderful time, and I'm sure it will be hard for her to get on that plane this evening to return home. Maybe I'll have a son-in-law soon. A golf pro son-in-law. Love you, TJ!

I have a Dr. Bevers appointment tomorrow. Always nervous about the CA-125 test and the pelvic exam. I pray that all is okay. I have had some discomfort in the lower abdomen, so I hope it is only something minor. I'm sure there will be a PET scan soon. Lani will be going with me since Bill is still sidelined. I will inform everyone tomorrow on the results. Just keep praying my friends.

Have a wonderful week. Hugs!

Ride, Baby, Ride!

July 18, 2012

Great news everyone. CA-125 was a 4. Pelvic and rectal exam were fine too—as far as being probed goes! I will have a PET scan within the next two weeks to put the icing on the cake and ensure that all is A-OK from the inside. Keep a clear PET scan in your prayers. The prayers sure worked for the CA-125.

Have a wonderful week everyone.

Ride, Baby, Ride!

July 23, 2012

Thank you to all who attended the jewelry fundraiser on Saturday. Everyone had a great time. Lots of wine and some hilarious photos taken. Some pictures are posted on Facebook. Seems my wig was the hit of the show. I even had bald men trying it on. FYI…clothing stayed on. For those of you who bought jewelry from Tajana, she thanks you. For those who listened to my little speech on ovarian cancer and bought books, I thank you. And for those who gave donations to the Leilani Essary Hurles Ovarian Cancer Research Fund, MD Anderson, Dr. Bevers, and I thank you very much! And to my good friends David and Linda, thanks for coming so far to attend. Dave, you're a real trooper to Bill-and-Magoo-sit! I'm sure the alcohol helped!

I took Bill out on his first out-of-the-house excursion. We drove to the bank, went to the post office, he bought his lottery tickets, and we had lunch at Dekker's. Had the catfish and gumbo…it was delicious. Bill actually stayed awake the whole time. He crashed the minute we hit the door of the house. And I hit the Merlot. OMG...it was like babysitting. I sit down with my wine and Magoo calls me over the intercom. I go to the monitor and he is running around his house "buck naked." He was getting ready to take a shower and wanted me to make sure he had enough soap. I told him, "If you don't have enough bar soap, use shampoo or toothpaste if you have to. I'll bring whatever you need after you dress." Picture this... ninety-eight...buck naked...walker...and I'm praying... please, don't bend over!

I finished a really great book. My friend and editor, Tyler Tichelaar, wrote it. It's titled *Spirit of the North*...and if you enjoy a talented author, an amazing story, and a few visits from spirits, you will enjoy this book. You can order it from his website **www.MarquetteFiction.com** or any bookstore. ENJOY!

Other than that, I'm a little confused. I thought my CA-125 was a 4, but I got a call today from MD Anderson and they said it is a 4.7, which to me is closer to a 5. I get awfully jumpy when it starts to rise. I have a PET scan next Monday, so I hope nothing appears. Nothing...not even the smallest dot. After talking with Dr. Bevers, I get the impression it would probably return sooner than last time...which puts us around next January or so. I pray not sooner, or better yet...not at all. Also next month, I have the breast MRI due to being BRCA 2 positive. If I had known all of this four years ago, I would not have any female parts and no ta-tas.. It's not worth it. Keep prayers coming!

Ride, Baby, Ride!

July 30, 2012

I Hate It!...I Hate It! But I endured the ride through the ultimate "brown panty" adventure. The horrid PET scan! Better known as nuclear wipe-out. I can thank my wonderful team at St. Luke's PET imaging for making my morning as uneventful as possible. Dawn, Leo, Danny, and Eugene, thank you. Dawn always makes sure that my schnoz is as far from the roof as she can get it. They played country music today...which relaxed me more... especially when George Strait is singing the last three minutes of the test. Anyway...probably get results tomorrow. And you know me; I'll be a nervous wreck until I do.

Thank you to my daughter-in-law, Michele, my little computer whiz. She set up all of our new computer equipment for us. I would have probably blown the damn thing up. If it is a 5G network....my brain works on 2Gs. Which means I have an instruction manual in one hand and a glass of wine in the other. Adrienne at Verizon...you are a peach. Thanks for putting up with two ole farts so early in the day. I just got through with my PET scan when we invaded Verizon and asked all the stupid questions that only we—the sixty-and-over crowd can ask. And no matter how well they explain it...it's still over our heads. Not to mention, I was starving from fasting. Not a good combo for a woman just stuck in a tube the size of a sink pipe.

Magoo had another tooth pulled last week. Lani escorted his rear to the dentist while I accompanied Bill's posterior to the doctor to get an ultrasound and checkup. The doctor wanted to make sure Bill didn't have a blood clot in the right leg where they took out a vein for the surgery. And the horses had their pedicures done by our wonderful farrier Trini. Good Lord willin' and the creek don't rise...we will make it another week.

The ovarian cancer research fund has really taken off. Thank you to all who have given and to all who have taken envelopes to give. Every dollar counts to find a cure for the "silent killer." If you need a donation form, please contact me through this website and I will mail you whatever you need. I can feel the love, and so will many others by the time we are through.

Pray for all who need a lift. Know that you are not alone, and you have many friends through this website who love and pray for you each day. BIG HUGS!

Ride, Baby, Ride!

July 31, 2012

Thanks for all the prayers. Just talked with Dr. Bevers... PET scan results were NEGATIVE! YEA!!! Now I can enjoy myself for a while and see how much trouble I can get into. Blessings to you all for all your support.

Ride, Baby, Ride!

Family Photos

Mace Side of the Family

Top: Cousin Lisa Cashion, Lani, Cousin Beckye Gross
Bottom: Me & Cousin Sandra Cameron, whom we lost in Dec. 2012

Daughter-in-Law Jennifer & Tim

Lani & TJ 2013

Patsie & Mark Lockett
Family Friends

Casey, Lani, & Dusty
My three angels 2013

Moochie 1999-2013
We Love You Mooch!

In Loving Memory

Michele Polasek

Dusty & Michele
2009

We lost Michele on
January 5, 2013

Coaching in 1988

Lani 18 Months

Cousin Norma Lower
whom we lost in Dec. 2012

My Mother & Me (2 yrs old)
Modeling at Sakowitz 1953

Leilani 6 Years
With Favorite Doll Bobby

David & Linda
Cruising Buddies

Leilani & Bill 2012
Notice he's not wearing his hearing aids.

Leilani Cruzin 2010

Lani & her father Pat.

The Hanging Boob Box

August 6, 2012

Three times a week (MWF) for one hour a day, I get to work out with Bill. The Bible tells us God will never give us more than we can handle. I don't think the "Good" Lord ever got sweaty with Bill. (In fact, today I didn't even work out. I wrote my update.) This carries love to a whole different level. We leave at 9:00 a.m. to get there by 10. We wire Bill up with his heart monitor and hit the warm up routine. Then we hit the different exercise machines. Bill seems to have taken to the treadmill and bike. Then we lift weights…or do a weight routine… and then sit for a combo of yoga and stretches. All I can say is Bill is a golfer; what else can you do with the bird legs he has? In the yoga stretches, the man tries to reach for my boobs—the only body parts I have left that are mine—and he is messing with them. I don't think they have added a breast rub to yoga classes yet. But we are feeling great and the workouts seem to be helping Bill with his overall strength. It also seems to be helping him sleep better. How can I tell? He is back to snoring!

Our Aussie mix needed to be groomed. BAD! He is an old guy and has issues with arthritis, so we can't take him in somewhere without a major ordeal. Bill and I hit upon a company called "The Pet Box." They come to the house and do it here. In their truck, they have a hydraulic lift, bathtub…the works. So thanks to Edward and his daughter Leah, Moochie looks and smells wonderful. He is so happy. But with Moochie getting all the attention, Starr, our lab, got jealous. So what does Starr do? She goes hunting and brings us a trophy. A nice bird. And puts it on her pillow. I asked her, "So, who urinated in your sandbox?" She just looked at me and pawed at it like…"See what I can still do!"

Did you ever have that one mosquito…that one that got away? The one you couldn't find until 2 a.m. and you hear it. You still can't find it until you are having a hot flash and kick the covers off your legs, and it bites you on the bottom of your foot. I named him "Evinrude." (I name all skitters Evinrude due to some cartoon movie way back when.) I saw him when I laid the flashlight on his mosquito ass. About one-inch long, combat boots, goggles, scarf, World War I flying helmet (probably borrowed from Snoopy), and a newly sharpened proboscis that could penetrate a concrete pair of pajamas. And that proboscis had my name written all over it. Let the games begin! How many bites can he get in before I spray the hell out of him? I've given enough blood in the last three years that I certainly don't need it displayed on my hand. FYI…all squirrels are named "Chip"…all lizards are "Rupert"…and all snakes are SHOT!

With all the mass shootings going on lately…the movies, and of all places, a place of worship, I would like everyone to remember that guns are a good thing but bad when put in the hands of bad individuals. Without going political on gun laws and not going against anyone's religious beliefs…I would like to quote the Book of James. "Be quick to listen, slow to speak, and slow to become angry." It seems so simple and so right.

Hugs to all.

Ride, Baby, Ride!

August 13, 2012

What is it with "NOSE HAIR"? I mean, why at the age of sixty-one, are the hair follicles in my sniffer going berserk? There must be some type of connection to the chemo treatments. After chemo, the hair in the nose says, "Ahhh, we are rid of that awful drug that kills us….Let's grow back longer and stronger than ever." It's a conspiracy! I think they have a recruiting station wedged up in there and send out draft notices. And so many shades of gray, blond, black, brown….it looks like a clown wig! So now I have to clip wild-growing, free-range, nose fringe every morning. It's now part of the routine along with brushing the pearly whites.

Rehab is going fine. I really enjoy the exercise and the wonderful nurses who work there. Thank you to Sarah, Carrie, Cassy, Debby, Betty, and Cecelia, the cardiac crew who make working out fun. Last Wednesday, Bill was informed that his "barn door" was open….Good thing the horse was not leaving the barn! It was a little eighty-year-old woman who noticed. See, you never get too old to stop looking! I was teasing the nurse (Carrie) that she was the one who showed the old lady Bill's open fly. She still denies it.

My brother and his wife sold their house over the weekend. Not sure where they will be moving. Sis-in-law's mom has to have surgery at the end of this month, so they will probably move to Mississippi for a while. Then hoping they get back to Texas. And on Saturday, Lani flew out to meet up with Mr. Wonderful. It is taking both sons to replace her. She does so much around here to help out. But she will be back in time for my breast MRI. Thank goodness! Can't imagine doing this with Bill in charge. OMG! He gets so panicky about "girl crap."

I read recently in a book about foods that fight cancer that the spice turmeric is an anticancer spice. I thought I would pass this on because it is so easy to add to a meal. Turmeric and its active ingredient, curcumin, has many anticancer properties that seem to help detour cancer cells. Add a teaspoon of turmeric to soups, salads, and even pasta dishes. It is an inexpensive way to get the curcumin intake that will help prevent the development of many types of cancer.

Off to rehab now, and then to see a friend of mine who is having a procedure done today. That is if she is up to it. Praying for great results. Hope everyone has a wonderful week. And what about those Texans! Looks like a good group this season. I won't jinx them right off the bat. But GO TEXANS!

Hugs,

Ride, Baby, Ride!

August 19, 2012

In the past week, without the assistance of my faithful sidekick Lani, I have teetered with the thought of how many times Moses had to have cussed. This is something I may have brought up before, but it's worth repeating. I mean, if in my little "nothing" life, things get screwed up in major proportions to the point of grabbing the wine bottle, then how many times in Moses' life, (all 120 years of it), did that man partake of the grape? And…let it all out! I mean...parting seas and crossing deserts takes a lot out of you. Wouldn't it be nice if we could part the traffic on I-10? Anyway, if the words that I'm thinking or that actually come out while I'm trying to stay calm and organized are worse than those of a sailor…I can only admire Moses for his patience and love for his people.

My challenge this week is tri-fold. Dealing with Bill and his little toe problems and rehab woes. Dealing with Magoo because we will be gone most of the week. (Get the Academy Award ready.) And my breast MRI. The only remaining feminine part left on me is in jeopardy.

That is besides the "who-ha," and if Dr. Bevers decides he is going to close that orifice up, I'm definitely putting a "For Sale" sign on this body and looking for a new one. I mean…my only fun these days is who is putting more time in with the "ole coot"….Bill or Dr. Bevers? Gotta love them…one keeps it happy, and one keeps it working.

I witnessed a beautiful sight the other night. I couldn't sleep (like many nights), so I went to the French doors by my bed. I could see every star in the sky. The perfect night sky. All at once (like many nights), I saw a falling star. But this was the biggest, brightest, falling star I have ever seen. It crossed over from north to south. Traveling slower than most. You could actually see the flames in its tail. Then it disappeared in the southern sky over the cattle field behind us. I gasped…out loud. It was so beautiful and amazing. All I could think of was an angel blowing me a kiss. Then, I thought, "That's no ordinary angel…that's Mom." (It will be fifteen years in November that I lost her.) It reminded me of the love I felt when she was near me. The love that radiated from her smile. I knew there was that same love radiating from that star. No matter what happens in my life, I will never fear anything, for I know I felt that glowing love star.

Magoo has learned the ups and downs of laundry duty. I have taught him well. But he had not experienced the sock bandit until last night. A navy sock was eaten by the washing machine masked man. Dad, it's a proven fact the washing machine eats articles of clothing. He asked me, "What can we do about it?" Make out a police report, take agitator DNA, let me know and I'll blast the S.O.B. with my 9mm…OMG, how about a scavenger hunt? Bingo, found and identified. Fell out of his PJs pants. Mental ward is not too far away. No, not for him…ME!

Friends are the key to life, and Bill and I got to have lunch with one of my best girlfriends after his rehab last Friday. So to Patricia H., better known as the "Bama King," we had a blast. Pat will be retiring at the end of this year, so we plan to make more time together. Also met a new friend, Robin C., a patient at MD Anderson of the incredibly handsome Dr. Bevers. (He'll owe me for that one!) Robin bought four books from me, and we plan on getting together in the future for her fundraiser. I'll get all the details out to you when I get them. She is in the middle of her chemo now...with the same side effects that all who have been through the poisoning know all so well.

I'll leave you with my thought of the day (Don't ask; it just pops up.)….Forgive your enemy, but don't forget his name!

Hugs,

Ride, Baby, Ride!

The Hanging Boob Box

August 25, 2012

I was going to write this earlier, but I still have not received the results from my Breast MRI. So I will get this off my chest…ha ha. Nothing I have done in my entire life of enduring all kinds of pain has ever been so uncomfortable. First, you have to climb your naked ass (undies only) up on the conveyor belt. Face Down! Then you situate your boobs in a box. The big box has two little boxes in it. Each little box gets a boob. And they just hang! Then you place your face in a hole that resembles what you use when getting a massage. Except it's only about 3" deep. So you are re-breathing the same air for one hour. Then you are deposited, feet first, in the tube. They say it takes forty-five minutes for the test. More like one hour. And YOU CANNOT MOVE! The noise is so loud and annoying. The only good thing about the noise is that it is so loud that you forget you can't breathe. You have a frame that your breastbone and diaphragm rest on…but what about people with ports? It is so painful to keep pressing on that area. One of Bill's rehab nurses, Betty, says that now I know what a cow feels like when she is being milked on one of the milking machines. The whole procedure is utterly ridiculous!

So, hopefully, I'll hear something soon, and I will be sure to pass it on. I figure it has to be good news. You would think that if they found something, I would have heard something right away. Anyway, for those of you who need a breast MRI in the future, get wasted before you go in, ask for a strong sedative, take naked pictures of George Strait to put in your face hole, have someone waiting for you when you get out with a bottle of wine, and pray that no one sees the images of your tits hanging through the rack. Not to mention your underwear ass facing the ceiling.

Ride, Baby, Ride!

August 27, 2012

Picture this…1:30 a.m.…not a creature was stirring except for Bill. The man actually fell out of bed. I mean rolled right off. FOR REAL! It was the loudest thud you have ever heard. Then a bang. Not only did he roll off the bed, but he hit his noggin on the way down. After I made sure he was okay, I cracked up. I have never seen that in my life. Not even during the drunken college days. It was like watching the Three Stooges. Want to know what the difference between my Jeep and Bill is? Bill doesn't have roll bars! The dogs looked at me like, "Is he sleeping down here with us?" It's a wonder Moochie wasn't snoozing right by Bill. He chose to honor me that night. They like my side of the bed because they can see out the French doors, and I have a multitude of fans blowing on me. Then as if that weren't enough excitement for the night, the weather changed and a huge storm blew in. Our Lab, Starr, has radar. She picked that storm up thirty minutes before it hit. She hates thunder. The first crash of thunder sent her flying on the bed. NO…sent her flying on top of me. Now as we all know, I try to accommodate when it comes to unforeseen circumstances, but I was now stuck between Ms. Scaredy-Cat and the bedroom parachuter! Life doesn't get any better than that!

Sometimes, I feel torn about life and its obstacles. Like the characters in Mark Twain's *Huckleberry Finn.* Sometimes I feel like Huck—practical, full of good common sense, adaptable, and sympathetic. Other times, I feel like his buddy, Tom Sawyer—imaginative, a hopeless romantic, and full of life's values. Then, at times, I feel like the last damn Cheerio in a bowl of cereal—soggy, dejected, but still floating! That's how I felt after the MRI. Can't imagine being one of Picasso's women...with multiple boobs. Can you imagine what that MRI machine would look like? Anyway, I called today because I still had not heard anything about the results. All is well with the ta-tas. Nothing bad showed up. Now, that is according to the lady I talked with on the phone because I was livid that I had not been contacted. Anyway…headlights are still on and perkier than ever. Well, for a woman of sixty-one.

Got to go get a haircut from son #1, Casey. We'll keep in touch if something else comes up. Thanks for the thoughts and prayers. Hugs!

Ride, Baby, Ride!

Copperhead Chaos

September 3, 2012

Hate them...absolutely hate them! Only good one is a dead one—hate them! And this one is DEAD! We went to have dinner with our good friends Linda and David, Steve and Susan, and Steve's girls at Collina's. Stopped by and had a glass of wine with my childhood friend Sharon and her hubby, then headed home to watch the end of the Bama football game. As we were retiring for the evening...Leilani goes outside clad in her usual bedtime attire (which usually isn't much...I know, way too much information). Anyway, sporting only a Texan T-shirt and undies, barefooted, and headed for the outdoor fridge to get a couple of bottled waters, I opened the back door and stepped through the doorway. I was greeted by two beady eyes. I jumped six feet, and that probably saved me from its strike because it tried! I'm jumping up and down at 10 p.m. on the back patio screaming, "SNAKE!" and what does Bill do? He passes by the kitchen window three times, piddling around, and he doesn't even hear me. The neighbors in the next time zone could, but Bill, of course, does not have his hearing equipment in. He has them in now...just not in his ears! Lani comes running with her camera (she heard me) and we retrieved two shovels to attack. Definitely a time for new underwear! The copperhead was about 3-4 feet long, nasty, ugly, scary, and very disturbing on one's bowels! I guess he was looking for frogs because he was right under the door, headed for the corner where our frog family lives.

Hope the little family is still in residence. Bill chopped it to bits...many pieces...and do you know that thing was still trying to bite. Even dissected! UGH!

Adding to the bedlam, Bill, in all of his great decisions, decides to let our sixteen-year-old grandson borrow our chainsaw to eliminate some tree limbs from their driveway. Bill, what were you thinking? I guess grandmothers are more cautious about stuff, although more common sense and smarter also come to mind. Of course, all my questions were answered by "the LOOK." I get nervous when our thirty-year old sons are using it. Did you give him safety glasses? Did you show him the emergency cut off? Did you warn him how heavy it gets when holding it a long time over your head? All answered the same way. I even got the comment, "I'm not stupid." So then we get a call that Braden is now the proud owner of five stitches in his leg! And who went ballistic about it? Bill! All I did was smirk, sitting in my recliner with my "victory lap" smile. No Bill...I don't think you're stupid. OMG! Man for sale. Slightly used, but he has a brand new heart!

Several things to pass on to you. September is ovarian cancer month. And our color is teal. And what a beautiful color it is. Please wear it this month and pray for all our sisters who need a cure, and for those in the future who will find out the hard way about it. One of Bill's rehab nurses, Carrie, gave me an article out of a magazine showing that Laura Mercier cosmetics will donate 100 percent of the profits of its sales this month to ovarian cancer research. So please help find a cure. Buy the hell out of her makeup. To learn more, visit **lauramercier.com/OCF**. And please remember to donate to the Leilani Essary Hurles Ovarian Cancer Research Fund set up at MD Anderson. Let me know if you need envelopes made especially for the fund. Thank you to all who have already given so unselfishly. Hugs!

Came across a list of foods that help fight bloating, especially the bloat feeling that comes with the many phases of cancer and its fun times…like chemo and steroid use. Asparagus, cucumbers, watercress, artichokes, green tea, lots of fruit…especially watermelon, fresh ginger, and fresh lemons. Of course, a good probiotic is always helpful. The partaking of the grape is said to be good for you as well, especially red wines. So…"sip" into something really comfortable like a nice glass of 14 Hands Merlot. It's one of my favorites.

Ride, Baby, Ride!

Wear the TEAL!

Magoo On The Loose

October 6, 2012

I really don't know where to begin. I can only say I appreciate all the phone calls and e-mails trying to check on us. The month of September was a nightmare when it came to our Internet service. Living in the country has its advantages, but it also has its setbacks. One of them is Internet service. Trying to improve our Internet, we changed from DSL with AT&T to wireless with Verizon, in the process saving $30 a month. Only problem is that two towers were fighting over our signals, which made it even slower than it was. So being the wonder company that it is, Verizon and its wonderful customer service agent, Adrienne, refunded all our money, let us keep the equipment, and did not charge us a fee to discontinue service early. Our cell phones are with them and we love it. Then there was the matter of hooking back up with AT&T, the only other provider we can use in Fulshear Farms (unless we went satellite). Now AT&T says we are no longer available for DSL…we have to go to U-Verse. Okay, fine. AT&T says, "We'll get you all set-up by Saturday." That was Saturday, September 1st. Since then we have talked to thirty different people, supervisors included, and gotten absolutely nowhere. Then a couple of weeks ago, when someone was supposed to come out for the fifth time, we get a call that we can't get U-verse in our area. Now we don't get U-verse and we can't get DSL back because we have to have the new U-verse. Now…do you see what we have been through? I'm on the phone daily talking to idiots all over the world who have no clue what is going on. I really don't know how the company can be the largest communication company in the world when it can't communicate. One day, I sat down with a glass of wine (I knew I'd be on the phone for a couple of hours) and tried again. Got a tech supervisor in The Philippines! I BLEW UP! I even had the F-bombs flying. So they had someone test the wires from somewhere and they left the phone wires disconnected! So we had no land-line for two days. I could go on and on. AT&T sent us six surveys to ask us how they did. Get this… they sent them on the Internet…which we don't have. Now, who was the Rhodes Scholar who thought of that? Anyway, we got it back yesterday evening. Good thing; I was starting to go crazy…well, more than I already am. I was counting George Straits instead of sheep...not a bad thing...those cute Wrangler buns clearing the fence.

Our Vegas trip was a great getaway for us. We had such a good time. Bill won handsomely in three-card poker, and I nailed a $450 win playing Keno. Saw many old friends. Lenny and the Keno girls, Kevin in sportsbook, and Bridget and Darren at Spago (an amazing Wolfgang Puck Grille). We got to meet and take pictures with "Big Elvis" (Pete Vallee) whom God has blessed with a beautiful voice that sounds just like that of the real Elvis. We also went to see the Donny and Marie Show, which was fantastic. So for a couple of old toots, we had a blast!

Bill is recovering nicely from his melanoma surgery. He had surgery on Thursday, and we are nursing his 3" incision on his face. Lab results should be back on Monday. Thank you to Dr. Ahern and his nurse Taryn, who is taking such good care of him. He also had a small carcinoma on his ear that was scraped off. As for me… blood work next week and pelvic exam with handsome Dr. Bevers. Must keep giving the who-ha attention. And get my port cleaned by the St. Luke's girls.

The only other thing to report is we bought a new toilet seat for the master bath. Very nice…a wooden oak look. But it squeaks when you sit down. If you move at all, it squeaks. People hear you from the other room…squeaks. The dogs are annoyed…squeaks. Now you spray both air freshener and WD-40.

Magoo is still hanging in there. Never a dull moment with him. Lani was in charge while we were in Vegas. The minute we hit town, she left for Wisconsin. Do not blame her. A week waiting on him feels closer to a month. Had to put new skis on his walker when we got back. Lani said he drove her nuts coming over here ten times a day. I have no idea where he gets his energy. He has to have a power pack concealed somewhere in his body.

Anyway, glad to be back. Lots of catching up to do. Missed talking with everyone, and I hope all of you are well. Special hug out to our daughter-in-law Michele, who lost her grandfather. I know how much she loved him.

Ride, Baby, Ride!

October 7, 2012

I would like to give a shout out about a few things going on in our area.

My friend Shara Fryer, who I'm sure all Houstonians are familiar with because she's been on Channel 13 for twenty-five years, now has a radio show on KTRK 740-AM from 5 to 8:30 a.m., the drive-time slot for morning work traffic. If you are an early bird…check her out. A wonderful lady and cancer survivor.

And last but not least…my pastor, Dr. Dave Peterson, has written a book, and it is now out. If you need an extra boost, a shot of love, a blessing is headed your way. Pick up a copy of *Receiving And Giving*. ISBN #978-1-935586-72-2. Dave challenges you to discover how blessed you are. Remember, we are all here for a reason and we meet people for a reason. Your blessing homework just shows up in every day happenings.

More later, my friends. Love and help one another.

Hugs,

Ride, Baby, Ride!

October 9, 2012

No, not a story about a Native American. A story about the excruciating leg pain that seems to occur more often lately, invading my "dreamland" slumber time. There is no describing this unwanted cramp. I jumped up at 4 a.m. doing an anti-charley horse dance. The dogs scattered as I flew off the bed, stomping the floor, crashing into dog pillows, a vase of flowers, oscillating fan, exercise equipment, and spewing more cuss words than a sailor in a whorehouse! And Bill calmly asks, "Is anything wrong?" Funeral service pending! For those of you who have seen the right side of Bill's face after his skin cancer surgery… well, he now has the left side to match. Even Starr, our female black Lab, looked at him and said, "Honestly, you are like a four-year-old boy who shaves! Mom is going to kick your ass." I visit Dr. Bevers on Thursday. I will add the question of what type of deficiency causes charley to visit. Has to be something I can add to my diet. But it must go well with Merlot!

What about those Texans? We had a great time watching the game. Kids, grandkids, and daughter-in-laws all came by for spaghetti and football. Even Magoo stayed up till half-time. Bets were out as to how long he would hang in there. I guess it will be Green Bay's turn next week. GO TEXANS!

Bill and I will be attending a Big Brothers Big Sisters luncheon today at Minute Maid Park. It is always a pleasure to be around great people who give of their time and share it with youth. It gives a boost to so many children who need a little extra TLC. My dad founded BBBS in Houston over sixty years ago, and Bill and I love being just a little small part of what he created. Thanks, Dad!

Has anyone ever had to put up with "not so intelligent" relatives (in-laws, outlaws, immediate, distant, and so on)?

From all the questions I get from all of you, it seems like a topic that needs to be discussed. Bill and I have them... everyone has them. But don't let it get to you. Do what you think is right and worry about your own problems. Some others think that they are the first ones you should come to. Remember…as Bill and I do…we are a team; we decide things together—what is best for us at the time. Our need at times is privacy, and others should respect that. And to those who have asked…yes, some people are ignorant enough to call names and stir up crap…. Ignore it and go on. Life throws curves, and people deal with them in different ways. Either they get over it and accept it….You know, like take off your diapers and quit pouting, or smile and wish whoever is in need…prayers and hope. Simple to most. I hope this helps. Our days are filled with knowing that we have each other and you.

If any of you have charley horse stories, send them to me. Maybe we can get a few laughs out of "drop to the floor" pain! I'll let you know when I get my blood work and exam news back. Bill gets his stitches out tomorrow. So we will also get his lab results back at that time. Hang in there everyone.

Hugs,

Ride, Baby, Ride!

October 12, 2012

Starting out today with great news. Bill got his stitches removed, and the test results show that Dr. Ahern got all of the melanoma. The incision looks fantastic. Dr. Ahern is a cosmetic genius. The other spot on Bill's ear is healing nicely as well. My CA-125 came back a 4. In fact, it went down from last time (depends on the calibration). To make the trifecta complete…the pelvic and rectal exams showed nothing. All clear for another three months, so all results from under the sheets are great! Dr. Bevers wasn't even shocked when I didn't wear the hospital gown. I just threw the sheet over me. He would just go under the gown. He said nothing I do shocks him anyway. Wonder what he meant by that? I think next time I'll surprise him with crotchless panties! Wouldn't have to remove those, except they would need another entrance for the rectal exam….Never mind; not worth the effort! Have my port flushed out today. So I'll get to visit with my St. Luke's girls whom I miss so much.

Last night, I attended a function for the Big Brothers Big Sisters organization. Ladies from all over the Houston area attended. CEO's, CFO's, Presidents, Vice-Presidents, and so on and so forth from all the major oil and gas companies, major banks, private businesses, etc. were there to give support to BBBS. As a member of the founding family, I would like to thank BBBS for inviting me to such a wonderful gathering. I know by all the outgoing and dedicated people whom I met that BBBS will be honored to have them join us in our mission to help all youngsters who need some guidance in their lives. Whether it be partnerships, volunteering as a Big Sister, or a donation…all will help in our goal to navigate youth in the right direction. A special thanks to Laura for opening her beautiful home (her wine cellar and the life-sized bronze statue of Louie Armstrong playing his trumpet were my favorite things there) and to Mary, who co-chaired the event. You are both very special ladies!

Also this week, Bill and I attended a luncheon and picture session at Minute Maid Park for the BBBS. Channel 2's Khambrel Marshall (also BBBS Houston Advisory Board Chair) was in charge of the emcee department. Khambrel has been a wonderful mentor for BBBS for many years, and we really appreciate all he does. And Pres. Ron… thanks for all you do. Amazing turnout.

Still collecting charley horse stories. The ones people have sent are hilarious. That will be featured in the Monday update. There is one story about a husband who experienced one who sleeps naked. I almost fell off my chair. Just something to look forward to.

Hugs,

Ride, Baby, Ride!

October 15, 2012

The best way to describe a colonoscopy is medieval torture treatment that is literally a pain in the ass! And the prep for a colonoscopy is a cannibal's way of cleaning the dinner before the meal. I have had several bloggers in the last few weeks ask me how I made it through so many butt adventures. In the past few years, as all know, and if you follow my book and happenings, intrusions to my heinie are numerous and will be as long as I keep kicking. Part of my exam routine. Lucky Dr. Bevers. Therefore, I have managed to come up with a list of ten things to help prepare for a colonoscopy.

THRONE PREPAREDNESS 101:

1. Mentally prepare yourself days in advance. Lots of wine helps. Don't eat a bunch of stuff that takes days to come out and is considered a clogger, like cheese. It just makes it worse in the end. No pun intended!

2. Have a can of foo-foo spray close by. Not saying your poop stinks, but you are the one having to sit in the fumes and, hopefully, no one else except maybe the dog, and mine even left me alone.

3. Comfortable clothing. No pants required. Socks or house slippers if you get cold feet.

4. Reading Material: Depends on your taste in literature. But no short stories. You will be there a while so find material that will last as long as you do. Catalogs, magazines, World Almanac, Colonoscopies for Dummies, are all acceptable.

5. TV is a must. Position it to where you can see it from the "john." And don't forget the remote. But don't set it on your lap...for obvious reasons. Unless it's poop and waterproof for over eight inches.

6. Telephone, cell phone, iPod, iPad, laptop, and any other devices that can occupy your attention for a while. Again, do not forget where you put them.

7. Make sure to have a comfortable toilet seat. Bill and I are very particular about our seat. Soft and cushioned are definitely a plus.

8. Games, puzzles, cards...or get caught up on paperwork. Don't forget a pencil.

9. Scrapbooking. Hey, takes up time and you ain't going nowhere!

10. Some type of butt cream handy. "Chap my ass" used to be just a saying when one was irritated about something. Vaseline, Desitin, or aloe should be kept near in case of the "chapped ass" syndrome.

In other words, being crazy in this situation just might work!

I was so thrilled to hear all your charley horse stories. Seriously, I knew everyone experiences these cramps on occasion, but the tales had me rolling. So let's start out on…What causes a charley horse cramp? According to Web-MD, they always come without warning. They can be caused by taking statin drugs (like Crestor), dehydration, a magnesium or potassium deficiency, poor circulation in your legs, exercising in extreme heat, or an overexertion of calf muscles. Web-MD also says that when one occurs, you can apply heat or ice, do stretches, massage it, or take a bath in Epsom salt. Now, the only thing I know is when I have one, I have to get up and stretch it. My friend Pat says she puts ice packs on hers; another lady said her mom always brushed the calf with a hairbrush, and others say they just wait it out. Whatever floats your boat.

I will be nice and leave all names out. In the first story, a lady said that her husband sleeps in "the buff." When a charley horse hit in the middle of the night…he bolted up out of bed and started jumping up and down. Now, visualizing this next part had me on the floor. Buck naked, jumping up and down, arms waving, spewing words of disgust, and the "ole rod and reel" bouncing all over the place. She said at that point it was hard to tell where the charley horse was.

Another lady had a cramp in the middle of the night and started screaming, so her husband flew out of bed, grabbed the pistol, and was ready to blow her away, thinking she was a burglar. So here's a hint. Turn on the light if you are going to scream, and turn the light off if your husband sleeps in the nude! One dude was jumping all over the place and banged up against the bedroom sliding glass door and took it out while setting off the alarm. So be careful out there.

If you live in the Houston area, here is some animal news for you. Our neighbors rescued a dog. An 8-9 month old male mix breed. His name is Bowser because they found him on Bowser Road. He has had his shots and will be neutered soon. He is a camel color with a white spot on his face. He is crate-trained and housebroken. He seems to get along with others well. If you know anyone interested, please contact me and I will get the info to our neighbors to call you. This little guy needs a good loving home.

As for me, I will be taking in more potassium to ward off leg cramps. So I guess I'll eat a banana every night as my bedtime snack. Take a banana to bed! No imagination journeys please. I could have opted for a cucumber!

Ride, Baby, Ride!

Hugs,

October 22, 2012

Heaven help us! I swear this is why I love my wine. Magoo has been a "world traveler." And by that, I mean that the man is freaking Superman! His cape is an ordinary bathrobe that just happens to be about twenty years old. His superhero shoes are house slippers from the nineteenth century. (He doesn't like new ones…they don't fit right.) His PJ tops never match his bottoms, and his sunglasses look like they are aviator goggles. Put them all together and it is "the astounding Magoo"! He falls off porches in a single bound. He thinks he has to check on the vehicle inventory every morning when he gets up. So nosey… always wants to know who has left the house. He has the timing of a computer event calendar. He comes out right when someone is getting ready to do something. The man picks the most inopportune times to show up at the back door. He has now decided that peeing off the porch is better than wasting water flushing the john. Gee…hope the neighbors think so too. Thank goodness we have five acres, so no one would ever know what he is doing. The only peeping toms around are the girls in the backfield, and believe me, he has absolutely nothing on their bull! Believe me…I know. I have long admired that boy!

I need more feedback from all of you. Lani and I are in the last stages of our book. There are things that I wanted to put in the first one that I didn't know how to fit in the first time around. I remember one day after the "big" surgery, lying there flat on my back…not being able to move too much, and people coming in and out with FOOD! Not that I cared a thing about it a day after surgery, but I heard a nurse say to someone, "I wish I had a Snickers right about now." My first thought was chocolate. That kinda woke me up a bit. Then I thought to myself, "Self, I almost lost my life. If I had to be a candy bar in life…what would be my ingredients?" I started adding things to my "must be in me" list. Things, of course, that I like…for example, chocolate, almonds, caramel, and more "fun-size" than "super-size." You know, a candy bar on steroids! But then I was visited by my minister extraordinaire Dr. Dave Peterson. He walked in and prayed with me. The man had just flown in from a trip and stopped by to see me at the hospital. How unselfish and caring is this? My thoughts then went from what goes into my personal perfect candy bar to what human traits would I give me to add to the ingredients. Unselfish would definitely be one. Live each day like it's your last. (I really thought it was.) The ability to laugh out loud and enjoy the fun things we miss everyday by just being stupid. Patience. The power to heal others mentally. Strength to do what needs to be done, and the endurance to rise to every challenge that comes my way. So now I'm an awesome candy bar! I enjoy life, and I love, heal, have patience and strength. Plus, I taste good, no artificial ingredients, melt in your mouth and in your hands…no hard covering on me. My expiration date is what I make it, and people come back for more! So now what is my name? "Divine Explosion"…the orgasmic chocolate that keeps on coming! Would love to hear what type of bar you would be. Get back to me.

My friend Dave Peterson and I had the great pleasure of meeting our publishing coach this morning. Patrick Snow is a professional keynote speaker, a publishing and book marketing coach, a small business coach, and the bestselling author of *The Affluent Entrepreneur* and *Creating Your Own Destiny*. Patrick lives in Washington, but he had a speaking engagement at the Westin Galleria. If you are interested in any of Patrick's talents, visit him at www.PatrickSnow.com. Dave's book is available through our church bookstore (Memorial Drive Presbyterian Church, Houston, TX). Ask for *Receiving and Giving: Unleashing the Bless Challenge in Your Life*.

I was reading through the Farmer's Almanac for 2013. I'm always interested in what the weather is going to do. There were many great articles, but one was a page listing all the names of the different phobias. A phobia is a persistent fear of something or a situation. For example, zoophobia is the fear of animals. (Makes sense.) I found one for Dr. Bing…the fear of train travel is siderodromophobia. (Not a clue how anyone came up with that word.) Fear of women is gynophobia. (Dr. Bevers and Dr. Cook obviously don't have that one.) Anyway, they go on and on. So I guess the fear of the "who-ha" is twatsscareomephobia! Remember, fear is only as deep as the mind allows.

My friend Lynn wrote me an e-mail not too long ago in which she said, "Life moves on. We make decisions that force change in ways we would predict will go well and go with the flow. The ability to make change is part of what brings peace in the end." I really like it and thought I would share it. No guarantees; crap happens and that's just life. Peter Pan said, "Reach for the stars…grab the moon…and take off across the sky." That's me, baby!

Ride, Baby, Ride!

Hugs,

October 29, 2012

I have been visiting Quito, Ecuador this past week. No, not literally, but the replica of it in the form of Magoo's domain. I walk in the house and drop to my knees from heatstroke. His dachshund Lilly was camped out on the porch, which should have been a huge hint that the weather inside was not its usual comfy self. If Lilly leaves her life of luxury (except to go to the bathroom), something is up. Like in this case…the temperature! As I started to enter, she started barking at me…DON'T GO IN THERE! The city on the equator had nothing on Magoo. And the man was in his recliner, watching TV in his famous 1920s bathrobe and drinking a Dr. Pepper. "Dad," I asked, "aren't you a little warm?" "Ahhh, yes…it is getting a little warm in here." OMG, a herd of camels would be searching for water, and the heat gods would move to Alaska! The potted plants were on their last root and sweat beads were forming on the fridge. Where the hell was the oasis? I am almost afraid to see the electric bill next month. Donations are being accepted, and we are searching for a foster home for Magoo!

I visited my favorite dentist and his harem last Thursday. Dr. Kaestner and girls had the honor of fixing my chipped tooth. Don't ask me how it was chipped...I don't know. The "chipping bandit" did it while I wasn't looking. So handsome Dr. K got to repair the damage. I walked in, sat in the chair, and proceeded to spread my legs. With his wonderful sense of humor, he laughed and said, "I work on the other end, dear." Oh yeah, I forgot…I'm so used to who-ha exams…habit! I'm sure he is thrilled that I am returning today with Lani. She has a teeth cleaning appointment. Hugs to Roger and gang for always making us feel so special.

The Halloween hayride visited the house on Saturday evening, led by the Fulshear Fire Dept. The kids had a safe, fun, and candy-rewarding hayride. Our neighborhood is so lucky to have this special event for the kids. Bill did not have to dress up this year to scare the crap out of them. He had his scar from his skin cancer surgery to amuse them. Actually, it's looking quite well—getting rid of the Frankenstein appearance. Our daughter-in-law Jennifer and our grandkids, Karleigh and Braden, joined us for the day to watch football and hand out the goodies. Braden helped Bill with all the outdoor chores. Mowing, weed-eating, and all the stuff that goes with five acres gets a little difficult for us old guys sometimes, so the help is always welcome.

Do you remember what it was like to have to go to the doctor when you were young? Didn't want to get that shot. Cried when you found out that was where you were headed. Mom tricked us into getting into the car… locked us in so there was no escape…and worst of all, bribed us with going out to lunch and candy. Well, I remember doing it to my kids too. And yesterday, I got to do it again with my thirty-three-year-old daughter. Yes… Lani. I had to go to Kroger to pick up Dad's pills and grocery shop. Asked her to come along to help out. When I went to pick up Magoo's "medicine cabinet," I informed her we were going to get our flu shots. Lani is the biggest coward when it comes to needles. Actually, in the past she has passed out. But our pharmacist Steve H. is my hero. And he gives great injections. I didn't even feel it. Lani started sweating the minute the word "shot" came out. She is fine now. A few beers helped relieve the emotional strain. We have elevated ourselves from promising candy to promising alcohol. What is this world coming to?

We have a red-shouldered hawk family that resides somewhere on or near our property. Every morning, the hawks are scavenging the area for goodies. Field mice beware! And they can rid the acreage of all the snakes they want. UGH! It is so neat to see them on their mission. Determined and strong. I warned Lilly of the threat.... She may want to camp out near the doggy door on equator days in the casa to avoid an encounter. I have seen those birds with some pretty large cargo in their possession. Their talons are huge!

I have been reading the book *Heaven Changes Everything* by the parents of Colton Burpo. They also wrote *Heaven is for Real.* In it, they talk about what I have said throughout *Ride, Baby, Ride!*—there are NO coincidences. Nothing happens by chance. Todd and Sonja Burpo call them "God-cidents." Great word to replace coincidence. So my friends, God put you in my life for a reason, and I know that is so special to me. This is a special gift God has sent us, and it's no coincidence!

Ride, Baby, Ride!

Men On Duty

November 5, 2012

Always afraid that history would repeat itself in certain stupid things I've done, I am very careful to try to remember stuff that seems to float away and keep focused on important issues. Well, I've gone and done it! The chemo fog cannot be blamed for this one. That is unless chemo meds stay in the system and hide and then pop out every now and then.

Once a week, I give into misery and shave Magoo. This is never a pleasant task. There are so many factors to consider. First of all…if I nick him in any way, he will bleed forever. Plavix kicks in and it is a disaster. Then I have to put up with his regiment of feeling every spot on his face to make sure I didn't miss one whisker. Then it's the bathroom visit always in the middle of the shave to prolong the time I am in misery. And on and on! So…I am pulling what little hair I have out in my haste to depart. I cleaned up our mess and went home...only to find the next day that I had deposited the shaving cream can in the fridge—next to the apple juice. (Deja vu…. Remember the time I couldn't find the ringing telephone in *Ride, Baby, Ride!* after a chemo session, and I found it in the fridge?) Lani was laughing so hard. She thought that Magoo's house had gone from equator to igloo status. Being discreet, I put the shaving cream can by Bill's shaving stuff. I really thought he had already shaved that morning. (That's my story and I'm sticking to it.) I am fixing breakfast when I hear this spew of words that a sailor in a whorehouse wouldn't use. I ran! Fast! Bill came barreling in the kitchen with icicles hanging from his face. I just chalked it up to his somehow deserving that. Or he will do something to deserve it.

And he did! I need to mention that we need to keep all sharp objects and ladders away from Bill. I am on the phone with my neighbor when I hear the spew of words again. I know this time it was nothing I've done...I think. I mean, he was outside on the front veranda, doing his "honey-do" list, decorating for the Halloween hay-riders. Bill walks in with a bleeding head. Are you ready? He forgot that the ceiling fans were on, climbed up the ladder, and got his head tangled in one. He is fine. No stitches needed. My neighbor and I decided that men need supervision no matter what they are doing! Of course, I'm good, unless I'm storing things!

I ran into a health tip that I thought might be helpful. I was reading about the problems that go along with cancer. Many cancer patients report fatigue. And I totally understand that, especially after chemo. Ginseng seems to be very helpful. People have reported a great difference in feeling less tired. Taking 2,000 milligrams of pure ground ginseng root daily seemed to be the key. I know ginseng is also helpful for memory lapses. And so is lecithin. The reason I bring this up is I will be downing both of these. Maybe that way, one day, I won't find Bill's ass stuffed in the refrigerator!

Very proud of my Texans. Went to the game yesterday with Bill, Lani, and daughter-in-law Jennifer. Had a blast. Thanks to sis-in-law Libby for Magoo-sitting. It was heartwarming that the Texans were honoring veterans. President George H. W. Bush was there to perform the coin toss. He is getting to the point where he needs help to walk, but he still has that wonderful smile and determination that I always loved about him. Challenger, the awesome bald eagle, flew around the stadium during the National Anthem, and I don't think there was a dry eye in the house. It was beautiful!

Entering into November brings a great feeling of love for me. I love the holidays and I look forward to them each year. Cooking, the wonderful smells, family, going to plays with Lani (it's our girl thing together each holiday season), and yes, even starting my Christmas shopping. I guess I feel so blessed to have the three extra Christmas seasons that God has given me.

Hugs,

Ride, Baby, Ride!

November 12, 2012

All the way to lunch with Bill in tow, I was so excited. Kinda like when your soufflé doesn't fall or when your dinner is ready in the Crockpot when you get home. (Erma Bombeck, my heroine, said somewhere in one of her books, "Don't ever let the sun set on an empty Crockpot.") I feel like I'm finally coming together after way too many months filled with bypasses, check-ups, heart rehabs, and so forth. No longer do I care what I look like when my fat ass passes a mirror. Everything now is focused on the holidays and fun, fun, fun. I'm looking forward to spending time with Lani in the kitchen, pretending we are master chefs, and drinking our wine while we concoct our famous feast.

Being a tomboy, of sorts, growing up, I never was real comfortable with all the domestic crap. Of course, all that came to a screeching halt when motherhood arrived. But I would much rather, as a teen, be in the swimming pool or riding my favorite horse at Lakeside Country Club (when they still had stables). And what a great time we are having as a family now. My kids are all happy, working, and actually talking to me. And by that, I mean… remember when kids were at the age when they didn't want anything to do with you. Wouldn't talk to you because parents weren't cool. And heaven forbid that they would be in the same room with you if one of their pals showed up! So, now I'm feeling on top of the world. I'm so spunky that I'm getting ready to do a few changes to the house.

Bill always says that my eyes start to sparkle when I'm up to something. I can't help it. My mind goes into gear and then that's it. Well, I've decided the kitchen needs an addition—a TV addition—so anyone eating at the bay window bar will be able to view the "boob tube" while dining on the "bird." The Texans play at 11:30 on Thanksgiving morning. If you are sitting at the beautiful mosaic bar that Casey made, you will not be able to see the big screen, which everyone else can view from all other points in the kitchen. Electrician Casey will hook it up and have it ready to go. The kitchen ceiling fan is nearby, so Bill is banned from the area when a ladder is in play. My non-domestic lifestyle needs football to help me make it through the day of hungry friends and family who visit the compound.

Bookstores are stuffed with discounts, coupons, and suggestive books on how to throw a successful Thanksgiving meal. Really? A $30.00 book of instructions on how to screw up my turkey? Some of the things they come up with…to do…to that poor bird. Isn't that why we bought a roaster—so we can stick Tom's butt in there and turn it on without having to mess with it? Isn't that why my mom forced me to learn how to make homemade cornbread because store-bought stuffing sucks? Isn't that why you open a can of Del Monte green beans and a can of the miracle substance, Campbell's Cream of Mushroom soup, so you can't fail? Then I see Dad walking across his porch. I think back on how he, and men and women like him (of course, there is no one like Magoo), made all of this possible. Possible for us to sit and give thanks with the ones we love. Possible to cuss in the kitchen over an "overcooked bird." Thank you, Dad, World War II U.S. Army Captain and reconnaissance pilot, and Bill, U.S. Air Force, and all the men and women who fought for our freedom...our green bean casseroles and a TV in the kitchen!

So, as you know, Moms have four sets of eyeballs. No, really. Mine did. And radar to go with it. It is an acquired skill, but it does exist. Ask any kid or husband. We have vision that ranges toward the north, east, south, and west. For instance, if Bill is in the kitchen...sink water running...then I hear him in a different room of the house, and I shout, "What are you doing?" and the answer comes back, "Letting the dogs out." I ask, "Then why is the water on in the kitchen?" He'll respond, "How do you know that?" PLEASE! Have you ever seen the TV ad with the dad, who after everything he attempts (and I mean the key word is "attempts"), always says, "Don't tell Mom!"?

Well, Lani and I fought the grocery store mob yesterday to make sure we had everything needed for the big day. I am determined not to set foot in a store the entire week of "Turkey Thursday." Men should not be allowed to grocery shop. Better yet, make them go to cart driving school. Every aisle where a man is left unattended with children, you hear stuff like: "Mom said not to get that," "Mom said that's not healthy," "Mom's going to be mad," "Mom is going to rip you a new one, Dad." Not to mention driving the cart all over the aisle. Come on, guys… it's like driving a car. Stay to the right. And corral your kids. Either keep them in or near your cart. Climbing the shelf to reach the Oreo Snacksters doesn't cut it. If dads had four sets of eyeballs like us, they wouldn't have to retrieve their lost brats at customer service!

Enjoy life, my friends. Reach out to someone who needs a little attention.

Hugs,

Ride, Baby, Ride!

November 19, 2012

As Lani and I were pulling away from the house, I casually said to her, "I don't know about this. Leaving four men alone, unattended, while we dine with the girls…. Kinda makes me nervous." Lani shot me the "I agree with you look" while rolling her eyes. But we thought of the bright side. We were only going down the road to "Ray's Grill" in Fulshear for steak and lobster night. Nothing could possibly happen. At least Casey was there with Bill, Magoo, and Uncle D (my brother) if something comes up. As we pulled into our parking spot, I could only imagine the 911 call in my mind. And the poor operator who was destined to receive it. We finished our dinner and wine with good friends, Benny and Carol….We said our goodbyes and they wished us well on what we would find when we returned home. At least we did not have an interrupting phone call.

But when we arrived at the house, Bill was standing at the side door. So, Bill is okay and in one piece. Where are the other three? Bill informs us that Casey went home. Smart Casey! And he and D had gone to Magoo's for *Wheel of Fortune*. And… "And what, Bill?" I asked. "Well," Bill said, "D went to his bungalow and I came back over here and your dad called me. He had hit his shin on his recliner, and…." "And what, Bill?" "And there is blood everywhere, and I tried to bandage him, but you'd better look at it."

OMG…it looked like a war zone. Who threw the grenade? The whole house smelled of Fabuloso. No…a Fabuloso factory. Why didn't I drink more wine at dinner? "Bill, Fabuloso doesn't take blood out of the carpet." Blood drops were everywhere. "Dad, next time you cut yourself, sit still." I spent the next hour cleaning up Magoo's phlebotomy cave. Isn't there a quote somewhere about patience being a virtue….Screw that crap! Henry Drummond once said, "You will find as you look back upon your life that the moments when you really have lived are the moments you have done things in a spirit of love." Well, I will look back on this moment that in the "spirit of love"...I didn't kill anybody!

Does everyone have the same aggravation with the metric system that I do? The scales at the doctor's office and hospitals are now in metrics. The nurse says, "Let's see what you weigh." No, let's not! I mean you get your fat butt up there and it reads 70. 70? What the hell does that mean? I haven't weighed 70 since I was in third grade. In actuality, that means you are too friggin' fat! Why can't a word just pop up? Like "too skinny," "average," or "Get your fat ass off of me; you're going to break my digital system computer." I guess this means I'm stuck somewhere between the lack of estrogen stage and the death stage. So at this age, we are just trying to stay in the holding pattern. You know...your shirts are dying from hot flash sweat. You want to punch someone out if he asks, "Are you cold?" Does this shirt look like I'm cold? It's really the "metallic group" age. Where we should live by the Periodic Chart of Elements. We have silver hair, take Silver Centrum vitamins, put gold in our teeth and bridges, carry a metal cane, have steel-toed shoes, (Bill needs steel protection everywhere especially when he's on a mission with the ladder), and we take Zinc for our colds.

We are at a time where you can advertise anything on TV or billboards. I always thought the feminine hygiene product commercials were disgusting. Have you ever passed a billboard on I-10 and there is a ten-foot tampon talking to you? Saying something like, "I can do everything but answer the phone." As women are complaining about having to go through that time of month (every month), men are about to run off the freeway, thinking about where the talking tampon is inserted. Bless their hearts. Even though I no longer require the service of the talking tampon, if they ever invent them to vibrate... look me up!

Starting to get ready for Turkey Day. I have used, abused, and worn out Mr. Clean. And I don't even know his first name. It's about time we were on a first name basis. All the Yankee Candle scents are just amazing. I bought two to go with all of Mr. Clean's hard work. "Farmer's Market" and "Spiced Pumpkin." Give them a try.

They must have a school somewhere for "assholes." Asshole classes. Not the orifice between your two cheeks, but the nasty people who are determined to be mean. Logic says being an asshole is not an illness...it's an acquired option. So I went on a counting assholes hunt. I woke up and said to myself, "Self, we are going to count assholes today. These people are individuals who deliberately, or not, cause other people mental stress. First of all, they come in all shapes, sizes, colors, and ages. They pop up everywhere. They really love to drive! In fact, they thrive on pissing off people on the highways and byways. So, every asshole I encounter I'm going to kill with kindness." That lasted through exactly four assholes and approximately thirty minutes. How do these people live that way? I just close my eyes and imagine them as a big pile of poop...and that just makes me SMILE! After all, it's Thanksgiving. And God wants us to love everyone... even the assholes.

Closing out today, I wanted to say that Bill and I saw the best NFL game ever yesterday. No one left the stadium, and if they did, they were sure sorry they did. Go Texans! Awesome game and awesome win! Thanks, Texans, for such an entertaining game, but you almost gave us all a heart attack. They play Detroit on Thanksgiving. Let's go 10-1. And SUPER BOWL! Thanks to dear friends Linda and David for going with us to the game. We always have fun!

Happy Thanksgiving everyone! We pray for peace, and we give thanks for all we have. God bless the USA!

Hugs!

Ride, Baby, Ride!

November 26, 2012

I do believe that we have all finally lost it. Thanksgiving morning started with rise and shine at 4:30 a.m. Well, rise...not too sure about the shine part. Libby and I met outside to venture to Magoo's to get the turkey out of his fridge. We could not fit another thing in ours...or hers. So twenty-seven-pound Tom begins his fate. Lani gets up at 6 a.m. and starts the Bloody Mary's. At 8 a.m., I am talking to the refrigerator. No…cussing at the refrigerator. The damn door alarm kept sounding because the doors had been left open too long. Libby is laughing at me while she is carrying on a complete conversation with her laptop. (For those who don't know, Lib is a travel agent and everyone was bothering her on Thanksgiving morning.) At 8:30, Bill had his first beer. I think it had something to do with being ordered out of the kitchen and a restraining order to stay at least fifteen feet away from us at all times. Then to get Bill really going, the girls decided we would hide his coffee cup. Don't be fooled. There wasn't coffee in the coffee cup. At 10 a.m. Butterball Tom was ready. At 11 a.m., family and friends arrived. At 11:30 a.m., the Texans started. By 3 p.m., we were all jumping up and down with the second big overtime victory in four days. It was a wonderful day. Full of football games, on TV and outside, pecan picking, golf cart riding, and guitar playing.

Then there is the after Thanksgiving fun. Hitting the grocery store for regular food and diet pills. Word of advice: Don't go shopping until you are sure all the kids are back in school. I feel it is okay to discipline kids….I feel it is okay to "water-board" brats! Better yet…let them grow up like we did. Not with these wussy parents they have now, but with Magoo! I would have rather been waterboarded. One look.from him would send those kids to their room screaming for cover. I mean, I heard a kid say

"No" to his mother. And the mom just looked at him and said something like "Don't say that." WHAT? A "No" would have put me in a coma for days. I really believe if I had the balls to say, "No" to Magoo today, I would be emergency room bound. What happened to the parental guts? I would definitely rank some of these kids right up there with Hitler, Son of Sam, and Manson. And what's the deal with thinking it's all right to get a girl pregnant right after you toss your diapers? I can't imagine, boy or girl, being a parent at age fifteen or sixteen. Greg Gutfeld of Fox Network's *Red Eye* and one of the hosts of *The Five* says, "Children are just tiny criminals"! I think he's on to something. Now we can't even turn them into "Twinkies Kids." It was fun to make them fat and harmless. That way they couldn't outrun you or Grandma when you were coming after them with a switch in your hand!

Our buckskin horse, Poco, has a new girlfriend. The jenny in the back field is his new flame. They meet at the fence and hug. He licks her ears. She makes her noises and all is good. I can honestly say that he has found himself a "piece of ass"…jackass, that is. They are so cute together. The other horse, Bud, just looks at Poco like he has lost his mind; he probably wants to tell him that she is just "fun size."

Ever thought about funny little sayings? Like…."How did you get yourself in such a pickle?" Or "Dumb as a doorknob," "not the sharpest knife in the drawer," "not the brightest crayon in the box," and "She eats like a bird." Well, I was thinking…how would you get yourself in a pickle? You'd look kinda funny in a pickle costume. How would you know which one was the dullest knife… try them all? What if the box only contained black, gray, white, and brown? Which would be the brightest? Eat like a bird…birds eat constantly…what an insult! Now if someone says, "He's hung like a bull," I expect an e-mail with detailed pics.

I saw a commercial on TV. The Charmin ad where the three bears are the stars. Momma Bear is doing laundry and finds "skid marks" in baby bears briefs. Papa Bear is playing X-box in the den. The point is: Why do laundry if they all are running around naked? The bears are bare! None of them have clothes on, but yet poor momma is washing clothes. I mean, how do you know baby bear didn't wipe good if he's not wearing briefs? Just one of those things like the tampon ads that drive me nuts!

Will be putting Christmas decorations up this week. Already got the tree out, and as Libby puts it, "fluffed it up." I decided to be extra careful this year on what goes out. Two reasons. Having to put everything back up is a pain in the ass! And I need to keep Bill off the ladder. Thank goodness it's cooler and the ceiling fans will remain off. Now, if they would just invent rubber concrete. Magoo has decided he doesn't want his Christmas stuff up just yet. Can't figure out why. Either he is planning on leaving us before Santa gets here, or he's afraid he'll trip over everything. We have given up on his "life" timetable. Whatever batteries he's equipped with are still putting out energy. Barely, but tiny sparks still keep him going.

Hugs,

Ride, Baby, Ride!

God Calls Us All Home

December 3, 2012

Douglas Fir is a family Christmas Tradition. He is an 18" tall artificial Douglas fir Christmas tree that lights up his eyes and mouth when he sings and talks. And he can be extremely annoying, especially to Lani. So Libby, Bill, and I decided to wake her up one morning at 6 a.m. with Douglas. We cracked her door and set him in the doorway and turned him on. Lani was not amused. So we set him on her sink so when she went into the bathroom, the motion detector would pick her up and he would go off. Lani was not amused. I think the last words we heard Douglas speak were "Have a tree-mendous Christmas!" And they were garbled due to the fact that he was going treetop first in the toilet.

The holiday season is full of surprises. Some wanted… others not. After removing all the decorations from fall and storing the Crockpots and roasters until Christmas dinner, I started trying to locate my egg timer. There needs to be an alarm locater on the egg timer. No, it was not in the refrigerator next to the phone and shaving cream. That's the first place my wonderful family wanted me to look. (Check out previous blogs to get the details on that.) Anyway, the timer turned up in the kitchen drawer, upside down, incognito, just like it was mooning me. I was daring the damn thing to "ding" on me. You know, like…"Ha ha, screw you, ding." Then Bill… OMG…loses the gate remote. That, at this point and time, actually makes me feel better. At least the egg timer is easily replaced! Everyone was summoned for the scavenger hunt. We know it's somewhere on the property because he let himself in the gate. Still have not found it. Again, why don't these gadgets have a "Here I am" alarm on them?

My brother D turned fifty-nine over the past week. My nephew, Walker, brought over a big birthday cake. I left the three guys with the cake to go over and watch *60 Minutes* with Magoo. When I came back, all that was left of the cake was the outer edge. All icing. I mean this was a serious group of cake eaters. It reminded me of when Lani was christened and we had a christening cake for her. We got back from the church and our dachshund, Buttons, had eaten exactly half the cake. And I picked up after her for two days. These three looked just as green.

The horses have been put on a serious diet. Our farrier, Trini, was here to do their pedicures and said they were too fat. I don't think Bud was fazed by the insult, but Poco was devastated since he is the one courting the neighbor's "jenny" and is going through his vain stage. So…cutting grain in half and no carrot and apple treats. Poor babies! I'm sure there are psychiatrists for equines… somewhere. Then Magoo's dog, Lilly, was chewing on something. She tried to hide it in her blanket. I asked her what she had. She looked straight at the corner of the couch. Then she looked down at the corner of the coffee table. In about ten strategic spots, I found pecans hidden. Now, in Magoo's fenced yard, there are no pecan trees. So how did the pecans get within Lilly's reach? Being the detective I am…I see the huge crows flying over Dad's yard and dropping them as if to bombard Lilly. Lilly grabs them and then buries, hides, and eats the rest. Isn't Mother Nature funny?

Bill sat up in bed at 1:30 a.m. and screamed, "Hello!" Scared the holy crap out of me. Then he proceeded to carry on a conversation with "whoever." Ah, Bill…oh, Bill…he looked at me and said someone knocked on the door. "So you are going to answer the door from the bed?" I asked. "Oh," he said, "I must be dreaming." No s**t! Please, dear Lord, let me get just one whack in! Maybe I can put him back out on the ladder. Ceiling fans ON!

Enjoy every day my friends. Life is a blessing! Believe!

Hugs!

Ride, Baby, Ride!

December 10, 2012

Windy, chilly, and damp. Finally getting some "holiday" weather. I mean, Christmas isn't Christmas unless there is at least a hint of winter weather, right? I think Santa Claus thought so last night when the northerner blew in. Fulshear winds were gauged at 35 mph. Our 4' light-up porch Santa was nowhere to be found this morning. At 5 a.m., I turned on the outdoor Christmas lights just to find his red ass. Cleverly, I followed the extension cord to the front bushes. There he was upside down, looking like a pothead (in other words his head was in a potted plant and his feet straight up in the air). Rough night, St. Nick?

The kids all came over for our traditional night of watching the movie *Christmas Vacation*. Lani baked cookies, and this year I ordered everyone a "Griswolds' Christmas Vacation" shirt to wear. The kids think I have totally gone off the deep end, but that's okay. When I'm long gone, they will think back on how humorous I was each Christmas. One year T-shirts, one year matching this or matching that. And they will wish I were still around to surprise them every year with something different or stupid. Well, maybe not. But, hopefully, they will be talking about it with fond memories and laugh about how much fun we had. Maybe next year, Griswold boxer shorts!

Magoo had to go to the dentist again. He had been complaining for a few days, so I gave in. $645.00 later…I drag his unhappy butt home. There has to be a better way to handle old people's teeth. Dr. K and his crew are so good with him, but he takes it out on whoever is stuck taking him there—all the way there and back. Anyway, on the way home, I get no conversation. I try to make a couple of funny comments about his mouth looking like a drooping bloodhound, but to no avail. He was having no part of that. Then I tried to turn on Christmas music and get him to enjoy "Jingle Bell Rock." His response, "Turn that down....It's too loud." Hell, I like "Jingle Bell Rock." It's one of my favorites. So I started singing it without the radio. Then I get the look from a "Tales from the Crypt" character and I'm told I can't sing. So, I hummed "Jingle Bell Rock." The man actually put his hands over his ears! I laughed so hard. A friend of mine, Ronny, who is in my breakfast club, said, "Karma is only a bitch if you are!" Boy, is Magoo in for a major encounter with karma. And I hope it's singing "Jingle Bell Rock"...off key!

Tackling the treadmill again. Always a fun activity when you've gotten so fat that even your stored away "fat clothes" don't fit—I mean that bag of clothes stuck way back in the closet that is labeled "only use in case of emergency." The bag that you swore you would never see again. The BS (Before Steroids) bag. OMG! Have you ever had a treadmill tell you to get off and add more oil. Then a light comes on and tells the world your weight. The little "treadmill gnome" had better watch it. I'm really close to doing something abusive with its circuits.

Lani walked into the den and told me that it looked like the Christmas Elf threw up in the house. She has always teased me about all the crap I put out for the Christmas holidays. I can't help it. It's not Christmas if you can walk safely through the den. In fact, navigating with a glass of wine helps. I have discovered "box wine." The big box contains thirty-seven glasses of wine. It has a tap—how convenient—and saves money and shopping time. Of course, it's not your "14 Hands" or a Francis Coppola, but it serves its purpose...cheap and it's not half-bad. Perfect for finding your way through the decorations, Santas, presents, tree, and sleeping dogs, without using your Garmin.

Bill and I were invited to a Children's Cancer Fundraiser at the beautiful home of Tilman Fertitta, the founder of Landry's Restaurants. It was so gracious of the Fertitta family to open their house to all of us for the evening. Lots of money was raised for MD Anderson's Children's Cancer Research. Kids are such incredible little troopers. God bless them. And Lani and I went to see *The Santaland Diaries* at the Alley Theater. If you have not seen it...it is a hoot. Very funny and adult rated. It is about a disgruntled Macy's elf. Everyone and everything is made fun of. A classic!

Stay warm, my friends. Hugs!

Ride, Baby, Ride!

December 17, 2012

(Written following the Sandy Hook Elementary School shooting on December 14 where twenty children and six adult staff members died.)

I cannot imagine the loss of a child. I have lost my mother. But the thought of losing a child is unbearable. I will start this blog by saying that in times of grief and suffering, you reach for family or friends. In addition to all our nation is enduring at this time…I, too, lost two family members within six days. I lost my cousin Sandra to lung cancer on Tuesday morning. Her service was Thursday night. Sunday morning, I lost my cousin Norma. They were both my favorite confidantes and both incredible ladies. I will remember the things about them that made me smile. I will remember the things that made me cry. And I will remember their unconditional love for their families, their friends, and me. I will be lost for a while, but I know they are with God. I know exactly what each one is up to in the heavenly kingdom. Norma is painting the sunsets (she was a wonderful artist), and Sandra is flying around her family with her new set of wings. Oh… and the wings have OU tattooed on them. (She was a graduate of Oklahoma University and always rubbed it in.) I know the faith-feeding thoughts they left behind for us to remember them by are…beautiful, loving, caring, and full of getting things done and not giving up. At least not until their bodies did. God bless the families of ones who lost treasures this week and keep them safe and warm in your unending love.

So for tonight, please keep those who have lost a loved one in your prayers. God calls us all home. I will write a blog entry again tomorrow.

Hugs!

Ride, Baby, Ride!

December 18, 2012

After recovering from a very rough week…I am ready to head into the beautiful season of Christmas. It will be tough without two of my favorite people in the world, but life goes on, and they would not want it any other way. (I wrote a small blog yesterday on the passing of my two cousins…six days apart.) So onward into the hustle and bustle of the holidays, actually my favorite time of year. Parties, family, friends, turkey, and ham, Lani's green bean casserole and presents!

It sounds like the animals in the adjacent farms know that it's Christmas too. And how do I know that? OMG! During my morning ritual of letting the dogs out to roam the property, clinging to my cup of coffee, I am bombarded with the sound of dueling roosters. Seriously, the testosterone was running berserk. One would crow, then the next one. I wasn't sure how many cocks were involved, but it was extremely annoying! And as if that weren't enough, Jenny decided to do her morning hee-hawing at the same time. Almost like chiming in. Either that little donkey was pissed at the chanticleers or she wanted to grow feathers and join in. To add to that, the cows that Jenny is protecting were wondering why she was running around the pasture kicking and bucking. So they added their two cents. I watched the sunrise and drank my coffee thinking…Noah must have drank A LOT!

We were sorry to see my brother D and his bride Libby leave. The few weeks they stayed with us went much too fast. But they found a cute house in Kerrville. It sits on top of a hill and looks down over the town. While they were here, we would enjoy cocktails at night while either watching football or Hallmark Christmas movies, or just sitting outside gazing at the stars and freezing our butts off. The only problem was…there seemed to be a Crown Royal bandit on the loose. And for once, you can't blame me because "wine" is my weapon of choice. Every other day, a new bottle of Crown was on the bar because the last bottle was empty. So we decided the Crown Royal bandit hides until we all go to bed, and then he pops out with his straw and sucks the life out of the Crown bottles! Can't you just envision a pesky little gnome wearing a crown on its head with a purple bag of jiggers and straws in tote, grinning from ear to ear, reciting "Catch me if you can!"? I'm telling you…it does exist. A night vision camera sounds like the perfect Christmas gift for our home. Now, how do you get a Crown bottle in a mousetrap?

Is anyone else being harassed by telephone calls from security companies? I mean two or three phone calls daily. Messages on the answering machine to the tune that the FBI says there have been several break-ins in our "neck of the woods," so we had better secure our home with their product. Number one…wouldn't we know if there had been a break-in around us? All the neighbors know each other and look out for each other. A strange car can't even go down the road without one of us calling the other to find out what's going on. So to all of you security companies...Don't Bother! We have roosters, a jenny, cows, dogs, plenty of Merlot and guns! Don't mess with Texas!

HOLIDAY HUGS!

Ride, Baby, Ride!

December 31, 2012

Hope everyone young and old, and those in the middle, had a wonderful Christmas season. Bill and I would like to wish everyone a blessed and safe 2013. May your guardian angels travel alongside you, may the good memories of 2012 keep you going, may God hold and keep our loved ones whom we lost until we are reunited with them again, and may God bless you always! A BIG New Year's Eve hug from our family to yours.

I will post a blog later this week. Lots of interesting stuff has gone on. I'm sure you will find it quite amusing!

Ride, Baby, Ride!

Getting It Off Your Chest

January 3, 2013

Let's see…where to start? During Christmas break, we lost power for about forty-five minutes. The extremely high winds were unbelievable. Put that with the cool air and it was too much for the country transformers. My neighbor—without mentioning any names, but he's a fireman—called to ask whether we had lost our power. While on the phone, Bill asked, "What is that noise in the background?" To which our fireman friend answered… are you ready?…he had fired up his generator (you know the one used in hurricane emergencies) to start his coffee pot! We were on the floor. Not to keep the fridge cold for important stuff like wine and beer, but to make his coffee. Only in the country!

Now, Magoo, in the meantime had decided to battle the 50 mph winds to see why there was no electricity. Like it's going to be written in jet vapor across the sky. And he did so after we told him to stay put because it was too dangerous to go venturing out. But, of course, roaming the porch is one of the things he does best—the other is not listening—so off he goes! Picture a sailboat in a hurricane, a flag in a tornado, a Kleenex in front of the Jolly Green Giant's fan. Well, that's what Magoo and his walker resembled. His robe was all over the place. Kinda like Superman's cape. It looked like a missile had been launched as he soared by his porch swing only to be stopped by the pillar at the end of the porch. If it hadn't been for that, he would have plowed face first into a mole hole; not even the mole was stupid enough to stick his head out on this day. Compare it to a football player parallel to the ground trying to cross the goal line.

I know some things do not deserve recognition, but I'll throw it in anyway. I like sitting in my chase lounge to relax. I don't get to do it often, especially during the busy holidays. But I was sitting relaxing and thinking about cancer-related stuff (one reason I don't like to think too deeply). Worrying about family...husband, dad, kids. Thinking of friends. And thinking, "What if God calls right now and you're sitting here watching your husband flipping the remote from one channel to the next…clueless, that you are worried about the future?" What is it with that dumb remote and the male species? It's like you put it in their hands and they are in another world. Now, I'm thinking, wouldn't it be great if there were a remote for life? Push a button and cancer is gone. Push a button and there is peace. Push a button and you can visit friends and family who have passed. Push a button and your husband disappears and the remote is all yours! Hey, this is fun…I bet I could think of several interesting scenarios. Several would include George Strait!

Then I have Magoo calling me because his house shoe is disassembling. Get the duct tape. So, over to his house I go. I walk in his door and…people, I could have cooked a chicken in the heat! No oven required. It was so hot his dog (Lilly) was half-in and half-out the doggy door. Easy deed for a dachshund. Head and front paws sticking outside...probably to breathe, and back end staying toasty. Magoo is sitting in his recliner, messing with his shoe. He is dressed in sweat clothes and his famous robe. "Dad, how can you breathe?" I asked. He said it felt fine to him. Every flower on his poinsettia had dropped off! If there was any living thing in that house...it had bailed! I wonder whether there is a button on that remote for this?

Then one night...the rockets red glare, bombs bursting in air...literally. Horses, cows, goats, chickens, rabbits, donkeys, dogs, cats, and birds were going crazy. Starr (our black Lab) was under her pillow. One of our neighbors down the street had decided to put on a "country club" fireworks show. It lasted twenty-two minutes. I counted. Magoo came out, asking, "Where are the bunkers?" No, Dad, you are not back in World War II, and we are not in Italy. I put my boots on and went out to check to make sure the horses didn't break through the fence. They were not happy, but they were okay. Guess what the two men of my house were doing? You guessed it...snoring. Bill and Moochie were out like lights. I mean, even the vibration would have been enough. So I did what every good wife would do. I stuck Bill's hearing aids in his ears and sat back and watched the look on his face. Works every time!

I received an e-mail from a lady named Shirley. I tried to e-mail her back, but the e-mail address given was not correct. So Shirley, if you are reading this, please contact me through this website. I am so humbled by your gracious words and know what you are going through. Thank you for buying my book for your Nook and I wish you all the best.

Take care everyone. I hope you have a blessed 2013.

Hugs!

Ride, Baby, Ride!

January 7, 2013

This past Saturday was a very sad day for our family. If you follow me or Lani on Facebook, you already know that we lost my beautiful daughter-in-law to congestive heart failure at the ripe ole age of thirty-one. The Lord giveth and the Lord taketh away. Death is always a mind messer-upper, especially when it takes one so young and near and dear to you. Precious Michele (my youngest son Dusty's wife) was loving, beautiful in and out, a talented artist, and a real hoot to be with. Every time I walk into our den, I can just imagine her flying through the door saying, "Hi, Mom....Thumbs up, Bill!" As I mentioned on Facebook, Heaven is in for a real treat. I'm sure she has already rearranged and organized everything. Female angels are now decked out in "spiky heels" and matching halos. The banana bowl needs refilling and the Little Debbie snacks are missing. But in Heaven, they refill automatically. I will miss you dearly, Michele, but I know that you now get the best hugs ever in the arms of God. Earth hugs sent to you. Please keep my son Dusty and Michele's mom, Carol, in your prayers.

NO CLUE! The crime happened in the bathroom, with the shampoo by the bathroom phantom. Remember the fun times playing *Clue*? "Elementary, my dear Watson"... or at least it was easy for Sherlock Holmes. So why am I having such a hard time figuring out what or who keeps screwing with the bathroom? #1...you're in the country, so don't flush anything you don't want to see again. The septic ghost will get you. Believe me! Here are my few observations:

- The bath accessories in the guest bath are light blue. If they appear a different color or have an unapproachable smell, throw them in the laundry basket. THEY ARE NOT CLEAN!

- The hair in the bottom of the tub or shower and the drain do not need to be shampooed! Please don't shampoo the hair that has fallen out of your head. Make sure all caps are tightly screwed back on. This includes liquid soap and conditioner as well. I could probably make three wigs with the amount of hair that is down that drain...probably not enough Liquid Plumber in town.

- Don't try to break the Guinness Book of World Records on how long you can have a hot shower. How about this—long hot showers make you go bald and cause you to catch the "hot shower disease"!

- When you write or draw stuff on the glass shower door, I can read what you wrote later on…thanks to the soap residue. Some are quite amusing.

- Room spray is there for a reason. Please use it if you poop!

Well…my Butts"R"Us time of year is coming to a close. Football season has only a few games left for me to enjoy the derriere scenery. So I'll switch to cowboys in Wranglers for the rodeo season. I'm going to need a new picture of the back side of George Strait. For some reason, my photo of him has mysterious fingerprints on it. I'll have to get Lani for that! Ha!

I guess Bill and I are aging gracefully. We watched the New Year's Eve ball drop while in bed with bottled water. Remembering everything, good and bad, that happened in 2012. Loved ones and friends lost and new friends gained. Praying for those who need heavenly help and for world peace. I mean, what gets into some people? It's amazing to me that people go through life not caring about others or how they feel, or they only help people out for money. Then something happens to "them" and all of a sudden they need someone. And guess what? Who's there to help? Whether it be a life-changing event…illness, divorce, jail, or a car accident…all of a sudden, they need someone. Yes, we are praying for them too. Bill and I hope everyone has a great 2013. Go over life's speed bumps slowly and the ride won't be so bumpy. Special prayer out to brother-in-law Ray in Ohio, who is battling pancreatic cancer.

Hugs!

Ride, Baby, Ride!

January 12, 2013

How to begin? How to describe the emptiness? How to absorb the pain that lingers with your son on the loss of his wife? We said our earthly goodbyes to Michele on Thursday. The funeral home was packed. If I had to guess, I would say probably 250 wonderful friends and family. My heart broke for my son, Dusty, and, of course, for Michele's family. Michele's sister gave a eulogy for her and I gave a eulogy for our family and friends. We are going to miss that incredible smile and that unforgettable sense of humor that was classic Michele. So until our spirits meet again, Michele, take care of yourself and of my grandson, Daniel Adam. Heaven certainly has its hands full if that "l'il toot" is anything like his daddy! (For those of you who did not know...Michele was four months pregnant with their son. They found this out during the autopsy.)

Ride, Baby, Ride!

Hugs from your mom-in-law,

January 16, 2013

Getting started today with medical updates. Bill will be having a sleep apnea test tonight. He gets to spend the night at the clinic and snore all he wants to. Bill has had bouts of restless nights so Dr. Odhav wanted to have his sleep habits checked out. So today he has to limit caffeine intake, can't take an afternoon "power nap," and show up at the clinic tonight. So I have put a "do not sit" sign on his recliner. I know if Bill sits for five minutes in that chair, his ass will be asleep.

I had my blood work done on Monday and my Dr. Bevers appointment yesterday. Happy to report that the CA-125 was a 3.5 and my pelvic exam looked good. Well, I don't know if it looked good to the Bev…from his view, but it looked good from a medical standpoint. So I will return in three months for another blood test and physical. And here's the catcher…I have a hernia, right above my belly-button. It will have to be fixed sometime in the future because it will only get bigger. I am still having gallstone misery every once in awhile. So I was hoping to combine the two surgeries and get it all taken care of at once. Kill two birds with one stone…no pun intended! Surgery date pending since Bill and I will be headed to Vegas for my birthday.

When in doubt...serve meatballs. Swedish, Italian, Home-Style, and Spicy. They come frozen or make your own, which is a good excuse to open an incredible bottle of wine to sip on while you slave in the kitchen. Quick, easy, satisfying…kinda like sex. I guess it depends on how much work you put into it. (For anyone under twenty-one, let's put your parents on the spot and ask them what this means!) The "Crockpot," not the "crackpot" serving it, really gets the credit. And depending on your taste… flavors are numerous. Personally, there is a "Roasted Raspberry Chipotle Sauce" that is made right here in Texas—Fredericksburg to be exact—that will knock your socks off…or whatever else you prefer to shed. It is a specialty product of Fischer & Wieser. This all natural and gluten-free sauce is named Razzpotle. Other thoughts on serving ideas are to add to any pork or beef, use as a dip for chicken fingers, mix with vinegar and oil to use as a salad dressing, or pour over cream cheese and serve with crackers. I have even used it in wine pairings and tastings. Anyway, try it out…it's really a hit with company.

We have a Hurles remote alert. The remote has grown testicles! Bill fell asleep in his recliner and happened to be snacking on...what else but leftover meatballs...and he dropped the remote right smack dab in the middle of the plate. (No, the man did not hear it fall.) Scared the poop out of me when I saw it. Looked like the remote needed a vasectomy!

How long can you keep leftover pie? Don't know why, but in our home, sweets are pretty much a special occasion. Anything chocolate is usually eaten or given away…right away. This prevents the temptation and saves the butt some damage. Bill will eat a piece of pie with his coffee every now and then. I, on the other hand, not at all. Only sweets exception for me is Snickers. Do not wave a Snickers under my nose. Magoo is a disposal for any stray sweet that comes along. He actually hears it calling his name: "Magoo…here I am! Magoo…come get a big bite!" If the man figures out that we have had a gathering of any kind, he knows there are "hidden butt-expanding treasures" at the house. Magoo on the loose! Incoming! Pie alert! I can definitely report in a modern day science journal that ninety-eight-year-old minds have a radar for pie.

Take care, everyone. We are slowly recovering from our loss of Michele, and Dusty is doing as well as can be expected. Each day is a little better. The Lord has His plan, and we will pray that each day brings good things and lots of healing. Thanks again for all the prayers. Not only for Michele, but for my blood work. We are truly blessed to have you all near.

Hugs!

Ride, Baby, Ride!

January 21, 2013

At 5:45 a.m. on Thursday, January 17th, Magoo hit the carpet with a crash! The port-a-potty went head over heels with him. I jumped out of bed and bolted to the monitor, only to see a laid-out, carpet-kissing, rug-hugging Magoo. Not to mention the pee all over the carpet. Lani called 911. The operator asked Lani three times whether she was sure of Dad's birthday. Born in 1914…for the third time! The paramedics whisked him off to the hospital. They were almost sure he broke something. In the emergency room, we met our doctor, who informed us the x-ray confirmed a break. Femur has lost the ball in the ball joint. In other words, the femur snapped and left the ball in the hip joint. Surgery was scheduled for Friday morning. Bill was in charge of Dad's "rod and reel" (you know…the male who-ha), so urinal duties were Bill's. What a disaster! And we were not even out of the ER yet. In the meantime, we were given a room and Dad was given a little morphine for pain. Now, we were sitting there in disbelief as the nursing team had to revive Magoo from "flat-lining." He had a reaction to the small amount of morphine given. So then they had to give him the antidote to save him. Amazingly…Magoo was back! Hell…it wasn't even noon yet!

So the night before surgery, Lani and I were in Dad's room, nestled in on our couch bed, drinking our wine and playing gin rummy. Dad was spaced out on the bed and talking out of his ass, and his poor nurse, Harry, has his hands full…literally! Harry was in charge of Dad's "peeing" duties, which Bill was happy to turn over to him. Now, Harry draws the curtain and this is what Lani and I hear. "Hi, Pops! Do you want to hold it or do you want me to? Do you have it in? Do you feel anything coming out? Does that feel better?" Lani and I are on the floor! We had to bury our heads in our pillows so the entire wing could not hear us laughing. So what do we do? We get the cell phones out and start taking pics with our wine and Lysol can. We sprayed everything before we touched it. Don't leave for the hospital without it!

Back at home, Lilly (Magoo's dog) was so lonesome. She barked and howled from missing Dad. So not only were we sedating Magoo…but his dog too. We left the TV and lights on 24/7 and gave her extra time when we were home. Bought extra toys and chew stuff for her. So back and forth we went. Home to hospital. Chocolate coffee to motor oil coffee. Nice hot shower to sink splash. Nice cozy bed to sharing a couch with Lani. Heads at opposite ends so we had Lysol sprayed socks in each other's face. What a great experience.

Friday morning, we were escorted to surgery pre-op. Dad had stayed groggy since his "near death" episode. But again, amazingly, he made it through surgery with flying colors. Now the fun part started. After surgery, the doctor came to tell us that he had put in a new hip joint.

And Dad would be in recovery for a while and then back to his room. So Lani, Bill, and I go home to shower and get something to eat. We hadn't even stepped foot in the door when we got a phone call. Magoo was screaming at everyone and hitting the nurses. So by the time we got there, they had put "boxing" gloves on him. Large, soft, and white. Giant mittens so he couldn't hurt himself or anyone else for that matter. So now he was trying to get out of the gloves so he could pull every tube he had… out! Including the "rod and reel" tube! Now, Magoo was not only sporting gloves, but they had to restrain his hands. His legs were already restrained because of the hip replacement. Poor Magoo…he was crying for help. But how do you explain anything to a ninety-eight-year-old who is doped up? He didn't even know who we were. The doctors said this situation was very common among the elderly. So we had his pain meds changed and also gave him a "relaxer," which calmed him down and helped him to sleep…a lot! Which was great for everyone involved.

So now, I am physically compromised and mentally challenged. Kinks in the back from the wonderful sleeping arrangements and mentally stressed out! But hanging in there. Lani and I actually slept at home last night. Bill has been back and forth doing honey-do's. The hospital sent a "sitter" for Dad, so we did not have to worry about anything. Such a relief. I will update everyone as things happen. Please know that we appreciate all the e-mails, calls, and cards. Your support through all our unfortunate ordeals the past few months have helped more than you will ever know. But today is a new day and my sixty-second birthday. So God has granted me another year. I pray that He continues to hold me tight and give me strength to deal with Magoo!

HUGS,

Ride, Baby, Ride!

January 28, 2013

Oh, Lord, you have finally challenged me to the limit. I have done the ultimate "gross out." Getting Magoo to poop and pee on/in a pan. I really thought I had seen it all. Wrong! Ninety-eight–year-old "rod and reels" are a real piece of work. For all you moms out there, I had the pleasure of raising two boys…know what I mean? Don't approach the male equipment unarmed. You need protection of some kind. A shield, raincoat, mini-umbrella, a tarp…anything to protect you from flying residue. Only difference between a baby and a ninety-eight-year-old rod is the pressure of the stream! How can I describe this? The little guy's is like a fireman's hose. The ninety-eight-year-old's is like a stopped up garbage disposal. It seeps like when you flush a dysfunctional toilet. And there is no difference between a baby's poop and a ninety-eight-year-old's poop….it all stinks. One poop session at rehab sent Lani and I running. Now remember, Magoo is on a "puree diet"...all of his foods are pureed. Magoo waited till we returned from lunch, then let it rip. First, asking us to turn him on his side. Big mistake! You know it's bad when your nose hairs curl up and take a sabbatical. The housekeeping dude walks in with his nose safely tucked in his T-shirt saying, "Here's the spray for the dirty diap!" Lani and I were hysterical. We have laughed more during Magoo's episodes than any other time I can remember. What a hoot! Nothing like pureed poop!

Lilly, Magoo's dog, has not only been sedated like Magoo, but she is a friggin' chip off the ole block. The dog whines like him and goes to the end of the porch to see whether there is a vehicle in the driveway (just to see if anyone is home...just like Dad). Nosey! Then she goes in the house to find some dumb-ass stunt to get attention. Lilly has taken clean clothes off the table and dragged them all over the house. She has taken pillows off the bed and couch and dragged them everywhere. She pulled the blanket off the bed. So I think we need to adjust Lilly's meds...she is just as "nuts" as Magoo! Probably passed on by osmosis. Next thing you know, she'll try to pee off the porch!

In all seriousness, Dad is having good days and bad ones. He sleeps a lot and is not drugged up. Just plum tired. His Seroquel, THE PILL (as we refer to it), does its job at night to keep him calm. I think a lot of it is boredom. Unable to move his body from the hips down has to be uncomfortable, to say the least. Add ninety-eight years to that and a few medical setbacks like a congestive heart, teeth rotting away due to age, sleep apnea, macular degeneration, and prostate cancer, and you've got a guy ready to exit to the spiritual world. Anyway, we are hoping for quality of life and not quantity. So we have decided not to insert a feeding tube but to let him eat normally, which could cause the lungs to fill. Aspirate. So we decided on pureed foods, which I mentioned before, and thick liquids. So hoping for a quick recovery or a quick exit with no pain. Magoo begins his rehab today… ought to be a trip!

So much more to write about, so I will keep the stories coming. Probably add a few updates this week to keep everyone abreast of Magoo's progress. Thank you again for all the calls, cards, e-mails and prayers. Y'all are the best!

Hugs,

Ride, Baby, Ride!

We Have Lost Magoo

February 7, 2013

This blog will be short and sweet. My dad passed away last night at the ripe old age of ninety-eight. He had a wonderful life full of adventure and fun. We will all miss him terribly…especially his little dog, Lilly. Lani and I were at his side when he met Jesus. He had an angel escort named Sandra…because he said her name. This meant to us that my cousin Sandra, who passed on December 11th, drew the "short straw" and had to haul his ass to Heaven. He went peacefully, calling us to his bedside and saying, "Come see me for the last time." We spoke our love for each other and talked about whom he would see in Heaven, including his great-grandson who passed away in Michele's womb along with Michele, only one month earlier. Dad left this world with a smile on his lips, a legacy that is endless, and a load of family and friends who loved him dearly. Details are pending for a celebration of life gathering here in Fulshear. He will be cremated and will have his ashes here with us. I dare not mix his with those of Mom, who resides in her "jumping dolphin" urn, because we decided that there would be so much commotion going on in there if we mixed the ashes that the urn would bounce right off the mantle. After all, Mom's been partying for fifteen years without him! She will probably meet him in the Macy's in the sky and want to know if he brought his American Express card with him. Don't leave for the spiritual world without it!

Thank you so much for all your thoughts and prayers. Magoo is in the arms of our Lord and knows he is and was loved. From earthly hugs to heavenly embraces...we love you Dad! Ride, Baby, Ride!

February 9, 2013

Some things in life are almost too much to bear. On the top of my list is the funeral home. The creepiest place on the planet. Men in black, extra-large elevators (made with marble floors and brass handles), which make you feel you are traveling up and down in a coffin, a Kleenex storage warehouse (so much Kleenex in every room that one could build a home with the boxes), skin-crawling music, and dead bodies! Even the lady who picked up Dad at the hospital to take him to the funeral home was the spitting image of Morticia in *The Addams Family*... dressed in black and with a strange sounding voice. I almost told her, "You can't have Magoo." If there is one profession there is to be in, though, it's the funeral home business. They are making all this money off of dead people. Oh, I think I'll take the Platinum Package for Uncle So-And-So…that will be a cool $98,000. Yes, ninety-eight thousand dollars! Okay, so Magoo gets the "deal of the month" package. Give us the one that costs the least and we get the most for when it comes to cremation. This comes complete with a ride from the hospital to the funeral home, a box to cremate him in, a box to put him in after cremation, a ride to and from the crematory place, a portrait of Magoo (any one we choose), and free registry with the funeral home. Now get this… *The Houston Chronicle* wants an arm and a leg for an obit column. (Wait a minute; Magoo has an arm and leg, and a new hip joint that's not being used at the moment… just saying.) I think the guy at the funeral home said they start at about $1,200. You talk about robbery! So Magoo will have a registry set up for him with the funeral home. I will get all the details to you when I get them.

It is so quiet around here. Everyone is going every which way, doing his or her own thing, not having to worry about who is going to stay with Magoo. It is a blessing of sorts. We all have our own lives and things we have to do, but I didn't realize how much time the care of a father took from our normal routine. I know Dad knew how lucky he was to have us around him, but I don't think he knew how much it had cut into our lives . Now there is no longer a calling of "incoming" as Magoo makes his way over to our back door. Or the calling of our names over his monitor. Or the betting of when he was going to fall in the pool or off the porch. But I can tell you that we are all going to miss that, each in our own way, but we are all glad that he is in a better place with no pain for him. Now if we can just manage his sidekick, Lilly, the clone of Magoo. She is now Magoo Jr. She roams the property with one of us and is seeing and experiencing the world in a whole new way. The sedation pills are still used if we leave for long periods of time. Might as well just leave things on the floor…'cause that's where they will end up. We are now trying to figure out who will take her. Lani leaves to move to South Carolina in March, so we have a little time to decide. We would let her stay over there at Magoo's, but she'd be so lonely. And Starr and Moochie are set in their ways too. My brother D and wife Libby have moved to Kerrville and have an old girl of their own. Oh well, there is an answer somewhere.

I will be adding things to the blog for the next few days. I will keep everyone abreast of the plans for Dad and how to get on the funeral home registry when it is set up. Thank you again for all your comments on Facebook, cards, e-mails, phone calls, and prayers. I speak for the entire family when I say that we are so lucky to have all of you in our lives.

Ride, Baby, Ride!

February 12, 2013

Trust is Earned
Forgiveness Takes Time
Faith Is Life's Key

My mother always said, "If you don't trust someone, don't be around them." Simple. Distance yourself. The Bible says there are double the angels around us in God's name as there are of the devil's bad guys. Good odds that the one whom you will trust is the right one. The way I see it, trust is earned and forgiveness takes time. When someone hurts you or deceives you, it takes lots of forgiveness time. On the other hand, some people just have the knack to continue to hurt others through lying, cheating, and being full of deceit. In those cases, forgiveness may take forever. Again, like trust, stay away from the hurt and pain of someone who doesn't see the painting exactly the way you do. Faith is God's way of keeping us on the right track. A comparison...two railroad tracks...side-by-side. One track has a train that travels along steadily but slows down to enjoy life. Then you have the other track. The fast track. Where the train goes barreling along to get to its destination quickly. Not slowing down, or stopping to help others, or to view or take in the surroundings. God wants us to board that first train. Too many take the second one.

I believe that life has its cycles, its seasons, its rotations and plans. Each season or cycle has a reason…a plan for you. God has given a plan to you at that particular season of your life. You are here for a reason. Magoo was here during his season one to play out the will of God. Magoo was an Eagle Scout, fought in World War II, started Big Brothers Big Sisters of Houston, led the community, helped start Lakeside Country Club, raised (with my mother) my brother and me, and lived season one to its fullest. Prudent, to say the least. Now he has been birthed into his spiritual season. The cycle of hope and love. Magoo is reunited with Leila, his wife of fifty-seven years, his granddaughter-in-law, Michele, and his great-grandson, Daniel. Ha...all I have to do to talk to Michele is turn on my app for Ghost Radar. She is always messing with me. We used to love to do that together and torment the spirits.

Do you remember things that your mother threatened you with when you were young? Stuff like: "I brought you into this world; I can take you out," "Just keep it up," "Wipe that smirk off your face," "Clean that plate; people are starving all over the world," "Take the bus. I had to walk six miles in the snow to school," "Think about what you did; in fact, think about it in your room," "Now you've done it," "You'd better be home by midnight," "Clean your room, or I'll make you live in it," "And just how old are you?", "Do you think that's funny? I'll show you funny," and "I'll knock you to the next planet." That kind of stuff. First of all, what was I supposed to wipe a smirk off with? Mom, you lived one block from the school; did you need a GPS? Why do I have to think about what I did? It's already been done, and I love my room; send me there anytime. If I'm not home by midnight, do I turn into a pumpkin? How old am I? Mom, if you don't know, who does? I thought I was showing you funny! If I have to be knocked to the next planet, can we go shopping for things for me to wear on Venus? The funny part is…I said them to my three kids too. Just something about moms and their hand-me-down theories. And I always thought Mom had lost her mind, wondering, "Mom, where did you come up with that one? And good ole Magoo...Dad needed nothing but "THAT LOOK" and my brother and I went running!

It's really amusing what you think about when you are orphaned. Hard to believe both of them are gone. But only gone from season one. I will meet them one day in season two. So next blog will be on the adventures Bill and I had while in Las Vegas and a few funnies from the hospital time with Magoo. I never got to pass on the wonderful getaway to Vegas stories. You know Bill screwed something up…right?

Thinking of you all and wanted all to know that Magoo's obit is on the George H. Lewis and Sons website…under obits and his name Oved S. Essary. I have to call to correct a few errors, but the pictures are great. We are planning a "Celebration of Life" sometime in the future.

Hugs!

Ride, Baby, Ride!

February 18, 2013

There were so many things that happened during our Vegas trip and before the departure of Magoo. Bill and I were sitting in the terminal waiting for our flight back to Houston. I was sipping on a glass of wine and reading a book. Bill was sitting next to me…first mistake. He began a regimen of sneezes…a full-blown sneeze attack. One of the sneezes forced his arm to fly up and molest my wine glass. He knocked it all over me. I was wearing a gray sweatshirt and jeans. Now I was wearing a Merlot-colored sweatshirt and spotted jeans. So I got up, with the entire flight of people going to Houston, laughing, and headed to the restroom. I leaned over the sink and drenched my shirt with water and a little soap. Women were trying to help, and of course, asking, "What happened?" Especially since I looked like I had entered myself in a wine grenade battle with wine aliens. All I had to say was, "My husband" and everyone agreed that it had to have been a man's fault! So then I was bent over the hand-dryer. You know, the kind of machine that could blow a polar bear off the Arctic ice from Las Vegas. The kind that you have to restart every ten seconds because in that short time you could remove every freckle from your hands. So I am draped over this blow dryer and I look like I'm trying to make love to the damn thing! Yes, some idiot called security. Two guards come in to ask what I am doing, and all I do is point outside where Bill is sitting and remind them of whose fault it was. And could I please have him arrested! They were laughing, while admitting that it did look kinda strange. I'm sure everyone was amused but me.

Then we got on the plane. We had a great trip home and retrieved our luggage. Got in the truck for our ride to the hospital to see Dad and then go home. The minute we got home, Bill was in panic mode. "What's wrong, Bill?" "Nothing." "Really?" Ten minutes later, it's…"Don't get mad." "Okay." "I lost one of my hearing aids." The "shot heard around the world" did not happen in 1775…it happened in 2013!

We have decided to keep Lilly. Family decision. We could not let her go without trying to get her out of her depression over losing Dad. As you know, we had her on sedation pills…did not work. We even tried those with muscle relaxers…did not work. Now the vet says she has separation anxiety. Okay…now we are on separation anxiety pills. Lilly has a "shrink." Now I need one! Our only problem is keeping Lilly and Starr separated. Wish us luck.

I will have the boobs squeezed on Thursday. Mammogram time. And then my gall bladder and hernia patch surgery will be on Feb. 27th. I will have the internal specialist and Dr. Bevers both there. Don't mind getting naked with those two hotties working on me. I'm getting really low on body parts these days. Oh well, one less part for the cancer to attack if it comes back. I'm expecting a clean bill of health after this.

Our family would like to thank the staff of George H. Lewis and Sons Funeral Home for their wonderful care of Dad. Magoo has been returned to us and is now sitting next to Mom and Michele. I'm sure the conversation going on is priceless. I have him sitting right between the two ladies. I hope he gets it in stereo!

Love is missing people every single day, but knowing they are resting in God's arms makes it okay.

Ride, Baby, Ride!

February 25, 2013

I had prayed to make the right decision about Magoo's little dog Lilly. I asked God to help me find what was right for her in her depression over losing dad. With Lilly's footprints all over our hearts, we had decided to keep her to make her life a little easier. Making another big move in her life at this time would have really depressed her. And she loved us as much as we loved her. Our attempt to love her like Magoo ended Saturday morning. Lilly had been shaking the day before and I knew it had to be physical pain. Probably going out in her back again. Saturday morning, she had no use of her back legs and was having a real hard time. Our wonderful vet here in Fulshear, Marne Baird, and Lani and me made the decision to let her go be with Magoo. Lilly and Magoo are now running the streets of Heaven together. And God is finding pecans burrowed in every nook and cranny of Heaven's corners. I know that in some strange way the Good Lord helped in this….He does work in mysterious ways! Lilly would never have gotten over the loss of Dad, and I know that she is safe in Magoo's arms as I write this. We love you both!

Serendipity on my part. Don't ask me how these things happen, but they do. I have discovered how to disguise a bag of chips so no one….not even Moochie and Starr... know I have them. You know the routine. Go to the kitchen, grab a bag of chips, and every animal, person, or thing comes out of the woodwork for a handout. Especially Bill. And remember, he can't hear crap! How is that? Doesn't hear me calling, but crinkle a bag of chips and he is standing right in front of you. Hey, a new way to find your husband…I mean if you really want to. So the rule of thumb is to see whether the dogs are outside, see where all occupants of the casa are, and carefully take the bag of chips or candy…open slowly and quietly...

and put them in a baggie. Baggies don't make near the noise. Bill walked right by me. Moochie and Starr unfortunately smelled something, but they didn't seem to be interested because there was no sound. The only thing that I couldn't get past the dogs were pork rinds. The smell and the crunch are too overwhelming. If you eat pork rinds…you get the drift!

After the death of a loved one, I think one of the hardest things is removal of their clothes from the closet. Except for Magoo! It was like a treasure hunt. I thought Lilly was the little scavenger. Heck, she had nothing on Dad. I mean, you still remember things about certain pieces of clothing, but all in all…this was a hoot. Magoo never bought a "cheap" anything in his life. But everything lasted him his lifetime. The suits that he bought in the Galleria in the '70s were still being used. There used to be a store in the Galleria called J. Wayne Limited. It was men's clothing, and it was owned by my cousin Sandra's husband Jerry. Most of Magoo's suit labels were from there. Suits still looking like he had just had them fitted. OMG…the shoes. He even kept a pair of loafers in which Lilly had chewed a hole in the toe. I remember he wore those to the dentist one time with one blue sock and one brown. The dentist and us had a good laugh. In his pockets was everything from coins and cough drops to paperclips and beer tops. In his desk, we found scrapbooks of his childhood. His report cards from grade school…Boy,

I wish I could confront him with some of those. I seem to remember "I didn't make C's!" Too funny!

I'll never forget when Magoo passed and Lani stuck her head out the door of his room to summon a nurse. She said, "He's gone," and the nurse said, "Where?" And Lani looked at me and we both broke up laughing as Lani proceeded to tell her, "Dead…left this world… Heaven…with the angels." I know Magoo was smiling all the way to the pearly gates. He wanted to leave on a fun note…and he did…all except entering Heaven in a hospital gown instead of one of his J. Wayne Limited suits. Probably got a kick out of that too!

So, now with all of this behind us, we are preparing for my surgery on Wednesday. Have to be at the hospital bright and early, and surgery is planned for 7:30. Drs. Bevers and Sehorn will be working on me. Sehorn will remove the gall bladder and patch the hernia…and Bevers will take a scope and look around for precaution to make sure none of the cancer has returned. They are not expecting to find anything...all the blood work has been great. Probably in for a two or three day stay. But all the troops have rallied like they usually do, and all is taken care of. Dusty is moving out here. He will take over Magoo's house. Lani is moving to South Carolina for a while to be with "Mr. Wonderful." TJ is a golf pro and is working at a country club there. They are hoping to move back to Texas one day soon. Don't get this mama started....It will be hard. But this is what is good for them at this time, and we know where that Southwest jet sits when she is ready for a visit. OR ME!

Had the boobs squeezed last Thursday. All is well. Mammograms are such fun! If you haven't tried one, you need to. It qualifies as a form of torture. Forget water-boarding! Anyway, for all of you asking, all results were good. Keep the prayers going for Wednesday. I will let you know about the results and all the hospital fun when I get home.

Hugs!

Ride, Baby, Ride!

Put Me In Coach

March 4, 2013

On a wing and a prayer, we left for St. Luke's Hospital in the med center. Arrived at St. Luke's at 6 a.m. Checked in and headed for the prep area. The very first thing, besides putting an armband ID on me, was to strap a GPS monitor on my wrist. The nurse said she'd been warned about me…that I did not like to be confined too long… go figure! I mean, it's not like I have spells where I don't know where I am. But I had very nice nurses and even a specialist there to activate my port. His name was Bong. Yes, like he and Lani informed the uninformed Bill and me, it is pronounced just like the bong that you smoke pot from…or something like that. Great start…! I am then wheeled off to pre-surgery and get to hold hands with my handsome Dr. Bevers and visit with my internist surgeon Dr. Sehorn. No lack of scenery with these two standing next to you. The anesthesiologist met with me and told me exactly what would occur during the surgery. It kinda makes you want to get up and change your mind. Then she asked me to think of something pleasant while they gave me my "knockout cocktail." I told them I'd be thinking of Dr. Bevers naked with me on a Bahamas beach. Score one for me. Turned "the Bev" red! Surgery went so well. I left OR with four holes. A hole over the belly button where Sehorn fixed the hernia and Bevers stuck the camera through. And three holes under my right boob to suck out the gall bladder.

Now, I do not have "jumbo jetters," but I don't have small ones either. I have always taken pride in my "tassle-tossers." So I asked Sehorn, while he was putting three holes under those "puppies," "What is Bevers doing? Hoisting the tit?" Sehorn laughed and said, "Well, he had to do something"…and so Bevers was left holding the ta-ta! Amazing what you find out after surgery. It reminds me of *The Golden Girls'* episode when Blanche discovered that when you are looking down in a mirror, everything looks like double chin but when you are on your back, your face looks great, but your boobs sag to the sides. Anyway, gall bladder gone, hernia repaired, and NO CANCER in sight. I was up walking around that afternoon and eating a soft diet that evening. Took no morphine after the surgery and no pain drugs at all.

OK'd for home. Man, those are the best sounding words. God was definitely there for my procedure. What was supposed to have taken 2½ hours took less. They took pictures of the insides (liver, gall bladder, and abdomen) so I have souvenir photos. I was told to take it easy for a couple of weeks…like vacuuming is a contact sport… and no heavy lifting. I told them I didn't expect to lift anything heavier than a bottle of Merlot.

During all of this, we got a call that Lilly's ashes were ready to be picked up. So we picked up Lilly and brought her home on the way back from the hospital. Her urn is now sitting on top of Magoo's urn, and I imagine that she is in his arms…just like old times.

Then…the worst day in a long time…Lani left for South Carolina. Youngest son, Dusty, is driving the moving truck and Lani is driving her car. As mothers and daughters do, we cried the whole departure. The guest bedroom she was using looks so empty. But she is starting on a new facet of her life. A new adventure…only it's without me. I will be fine, and while in the hospital, I made a mile-long list to keep me busy. She will be back in two weeks for the George Strait concert, so the next couple of weeks won't be so bad.

Anyway, during all of this, Dusty is selling his house. Too many memories of our Michele there for him. I can only imagine. I feel that way every time I enter Magoo's house. But the good news is Dusty is going to move in to Dad's to help us out here. So instead of Lani as my guardian angel, I have Dusty. I guess like the commercial, Dusty will have to find the "snooze button" on the rooster. I will really enjoy him getting used to the country sounds! So he will have his regular job and the "odd jobs" ready for him here. It is so reassuring to have someone close to help in case Bill and I need him. Getting old is CRAZY!

So, as the saying goes…"Nobody better leave the gate open"…'cause this ole broad is ready to play! Thanks for all the prayers and good wishes. You are all very special to me. And the last few months, I have been reassured many times over how much the love of family and friends means. Hugs!

Ride, Baby, Ride!

March 11, 2013

I'm not perfect. And the Good Lord knows…I'm not normal. But the worst part of recovery from surgery is not being able to drive for a couple of weeks. After one week of being the stressed out passenger and not the driver, I was begging the doctors to please let me drive. If I don't do anything else on this planet...please let me operate a motor vehicle. Let's put it this way...one more week of Bill's driving would have been the end of my life as I now know it! I would have either had a heart attack, or I would have hired someone to put me out of my misery. First thing, Bill almost stops to turn. I wish I had a dollar for every time people honked at us. I asked him whether he gets this much attention every time he drives. His response was like…"What?" He doesn't hear them honk! I keep imagining my poor Jeep being sodomized by another car behind us. The man sailed over speed bumps like we had "friggin'" wings. He said, "They should have had them painted brighter." Any brighter and they could be UFO landing pads! There is an indention in the ragtop where I had to remove my cranium. We nearly hit a gas pump. Don't ask! And right before my plea to the medical board, we nearly side-swiped a truck carrying live chickens to the rodeo. An RV full of cluckers, a mobile egg-laying union of pissed off hens, which Bill honked at as feathers went flying everywhere. I had nightmares for days about my Jeep covered in chicken poop.

In my opinion, Mother Nature has gone crazy. We have cardinals, blue jays, hawks, mockingbirds, chickadees, wrens, and sparrows all mating. No concern about intimate privacy around here. Daddy Cardinal continues to amuse himself in the truck mirrors while Daddy Mockingbird is trying to mate with the den window. The hawks, I think, like to do it while flying. The others don't give a crap about where or when. It's bad when you become an expert on birds' sexual habits. I need a real paying job!

You must play to know how much fun the game is. You can't warm the sideline or sit on the bench and watch. You have to play the game. It's not...oh no…I have cancer, so I'll sit this one out. It's okay that I have cancer, and I'm going to play to win. God wants you to play the game, my friends. Have fun with life…LIVE IT! Today I am going to have a hole-in-one, a touchdown, a home run, ace it, take the winning lap, hit a three-pointer, score a goal, or beat the odds.

Lani has been gone nine days now. It seems like forever. I just can't think about it. Dusty returns from helping her move tomorrow. Our friends Linda and David will be over on Wednesday…so Linda can help me with the final touches of the new book. It will then go to Tyler for editing. So get ready for *They're Pistols and They're Loaded.* Real excited about this one, and hope you will all enjoy reading it as much as Lani and I enjoyed writing it.

So…put me in God…I'm playing today!

Ride, Baby, Ride!

March 18, 2013

I wrote this blog being of sound body and mind…I think. While spring cleaning, I took the liberty of checking all the fire extinguishers. Big mistake! I do not think God in all His wisdom put women on this earth to test the working parts of a fire extinguisher. Easy to use… MY ASS! Let me start by saying "Wear protective clothing and goggles." Instructions go something like this: Please make sure that you test your fire extinguisher every month. (Okay…this is the first time in ten years. I know, they are not supposed to be an art form just hanging on the wall for a talking piece…they are to save lives if a fire should start in your home.) First…check the gauge. The pressure indicator arrow should be in the green space. If the arrow is not in the green space, throw it out and buy another. Otherwise, with arrow in green space, pull the pin. Stand six feet from the testing spot, aim, squeeze the handle, and sweep from side to side. May I say…you really need to see where the stuff comes out. The right direction is a must. And be prepared for a loud noise. The instructions say nothing about the sonic boom when squeezed.

Since I decided that the best place to test it was outside, I picked a spot where I felt all of nature would be safe. The mockingbird decided it had to be a witness to this humiliating failure of modern technology and would not shut up. I was very tempted to show him/her how fun it feels to be creamed by a blast of whatever is in the container. Instead…I found out. I had that crap everywhere. The horses took off running. Starr headed for the house. The mockingbird flew right into the side of the barn (didn't hurt it), and I looked like I had gotten into a fight with the Pillsbury Doughboy. Only one extinguisher was tested, but all will be replaced. I will never test one again. Thank God I didn't have Bill do it. Winston Churchill once said, "A pessimist sees the difficulty in every opportunity; an optimist sees the opportunity in every difficulty." I don't think old Winston ever had to check a fire extinguisher!

I picked up a book, at the grocery store of all places, and got the biggest kick out of a small book about God and wisdom. It's by Steve Chapman and titled *Wasn't it Smart of God To…*" In it are some things that just make you laugh. And boy, I'm looking for things to keep my mind off the last three months. Here are a few samples:

Wasn't it smart of God to:

- …put our noses on our faces instead of under our arms—for odorously obvious reasons.
- …make the rain fall in lots of little drops instead of one really big one.
- …give us two ears and one mouth so we'll remember to listen twice as much as we talk.
- …give us two eyebrows instead of one—and tweezers to help keep them that way.

And they go on and on. I think I'll go back and buy a couple to give as gifts. A nice inexpensive picker upper.

Well, we have to share the not-so-good news with the good. We are missing Moochie. Our beloved Aussie mix entered his spiritual life on Friday at the age of fourteen. The entire family is in a tailspin. And I use that phrase because Moochie didn't have a tail…Aussies don't have them. When he was excited, his whole butt would wag. Bill and I made the decision to let him go be with Lilly and the other doggy angels because he had developed a vestibular problem. And that could have been a brain tumor. We decided not to put him through all the tests. We had fourteen loyal, loving years together, and we miss him so much. Starr (our black lab) is still looking for him and falls asleep with her head in my hand. Our boy is now with God and "mooching" scraps off the heavenly plates of the angels. We love you, Mooch-Man!

Still miss Lani…more every day. Dusty has moved many of his things in along with his two dogs. Chico is a Houdini…and has no problem opening the gate with his paw. He reminds me of our good friends Linda and David's dog Tanner, who does the same thing with their back door. Like we all say…now we have to teach him to close it! Dusty went with us to the George Strait Concert at Reliant Stadium last night. King George did it again. Eighty-thousand-plus people to see his farewell tour show. Only thing missing was my sidekick…Lani.

I received many funny stories about men driving their wives from you all. I swear, you just can't make this stuff up. Everything from hitting curbs, messing up the tires, scratches and dents, and having to take anxiety pills. I'll have to do another blog on this topic very soon.

Have a great week. Hugs!

Ride, Baby, Ride!

March 25, 2013

As we sail through this month just as we have all the rest, I seem to be getting vibes to do something different. I have recently (this past year) been involved with a group of people in the Fulshear/Katy area who meet twice a month; our goal is to help each other thrive through our different businesses. I have hooked up with an outfit that helps promote your business through the making of a video. So for the purpose of getting the word out about the "silent killer," ovarian cancer, I have decided to go through with this exciting adventure. I believe it will definitely be a plus for the cause. I will be talking about symptoms, my experience with surgeries and chemo, and living life to its fullest. It will be launched on Facebook and YouTube, as well as my website.

Bill and I are getting used to the granddogs that have moved in with us, as well as the coming and goings of Dusty. I had forgotten how much energy young people have. It's enough to make you inhale wine and not sip it. Starr is better about the loss of her beloved brother, Moochie, and seems to be doing better each day. I wish I could say the same about Bill and me. I just wish we could explain in doggy words what happened. Dusty's dogs help by playing with Starr and running up and down the fence line, but she will only play for a little while and then retreats back to the house.

Dusty is finding out what a "pack rat" Michele was, and we spend hours at a time reading her notes and comments she strategically left for Dusty to find. Quite a clever young lady. I think she knew she did not have much time, and now from Heaven, she sends messages our way. Daughter-in-law Jennifer and I were talking in the kitchen this weekend when the top of the trash can started swinging…and I mean swinging. No one was around it, and no fans or anything of that sort were blowing it. We both were floored! Then I was in the den and my Dean Martin puppet doll turned on by itself and started singing. Dean is on a dresser in the office. I was nowhere near it. Bill was out mowing, Starr was asleep on her pillow by me, Dusty was at work…so don't ask me. I think Magoo and Michele have teamed up on earthly visits to let us know they are fine. Magoo was always bitching that the trash needed to be taken out (although his can was almost empty...nothing near the lid), and Michele and I used to talk all the time about me having a huge crush on Dean Martin as a kid. Logical to me! Just bought two more cases of Merlot for back-up!

Our dear friends Linda and David are helping me put the final touches on the new book. We are gathering pictures and last minute chapter "info" so I can send it to my "main man" Tyler, editor extraordinaire. Lani should be in near the end of April for a few weeks, so hopefully, we can tie up any loose ends at that time. She will be here for the wedding of her cousin, my nephew Ryan. The whole family is looking forward to that adventure. They will be getting married on what would have been Magoo's ninety-ninth birthday. With Dad and Michele having so much fun in the spiritual world, I'd hate to think what they have in store for the wedding. We'd better pack plenty of "spirits" of our own.

I'm doing the finishing touches on Dad's final affairs. Letting go of someone is one thing, but dealing with the paperwork is another. So time-consuming and sad. My advice to anyone who loses someone dear is to hire someone else to handle the crap. But Magoo left happy, and he took care of many things years ago, which helped. I will always be in admiration of just how organized he was. We are still planning to have his celebration of life sometime in June.

Enjoy the beautiful spring weather. A little nippy today but beautiful. Feel bad for y'all up there in that snowstorm. My good friends who live in Virginia, Jim and Rita, had their truck demolished by a tree branch that broke off and fell. It was so weighed down by ice and snow. Kinda got the feelin' that truck was Jim's pride and joy!

God bless, and if you hear things that go bump in the night…just smile…Magoo and Michele are on the loose!

Ride, Baby, Ride!

Adventures End and New Ones Begin

As I head into my fourth year of battle with ovarian cancer, I still carry an army of supporters. The doctors are my generals and are keeping our strategies to win the war and keep me alive. My family and friends are true soldiers who have unselfishly kept my spirits high. Lani and I are so lucky to have the power of all these things to keep us strong and motivated. We have lost many who have been a major part of our lives and big parts of my last book *Ride, Baby, Ride!* Dad, better known as Magoo, beautiful daughter-in-law Michele, who was carrying my grandson Daniel when she passed, cousins Sandra and Norma, and our beloved pets Moochie and Lilly. So we thank God every day for His love and guidance. His presence has made us strong.

So until our next book of adventures, Ride, Baby, Ride! And keep those pistols loaded!

Leilani and Lani

Leilani's Life Lessons

- Life is about waiting for the storms to pass. It's about learning to dance in the rain. It's about having the power to choose to forgive and believe in others.
- You can't expect everyone to feel the same way you do. Wouldn't that make things a lot more simple? So my formula for success is to listen, learn, and be there when I can for the ones I love. Sometimes, that's not possible and circumstances change. But we all have it in us to accept what can't be changed and not to give up.
- Cancer has taught me many things. There are so many people in the same boat as me. I'm still paddling, but some are putting on life jackets and wanting to jump into the cold dark waters. Remember Philippians 4:13, "I can do all things in him that strengthens me."

- My mother would always tell me there are things you should always have an extra stash of. Your favorite snack…of course, mine was Snickers, toilet paper, lipstick (like in every nook and cranny), and an extra pair of underwear. Now, that one I couldn't figure out until George Strait touched my hand, twice, in one concert, and I only had one pair of extra panties. Listen to Mom!

- When traveling, take "Big Bertha" with you. Big Bertha is the huge bag that is your extra carry-on that you don't have to pay for, and into which you sneak everything and anything that could possibly be needed at any given time during a trip. We have through the years managed everything from gum to condoms. I mean, one just never knows. Even the TSA looks at Bertha and sighs…OMG! Don't worry; the plane takes off on time. When traveling in the car, you can even load the pistol in it. It's probably a Texas thing!

- Men can't help it. They just can't help it. I'm surprised my mom resisted doing major drugs. Dad was such a pain in the ass. The older he got, the more it showed. Mom checked out at the right time. Lani and I are forever rolling our eyes at the men in our lives. If one doesn't think of something unreal, the other one will. Never fails! They are just like little boys in bigger packages. And, of course, they have to have some type of toy. Whether it be cars, boats, guns, golf, the remote, etc. They always have to be into something that they can use as an excuse when they are late or making up for something they were supposed to be doing but got sidetracked and forgot to do.

A Giving Thought

Life has its way of throwing some major surprises your way. A "lifequake" of major magnitude jolted my world when I was diagnosed with life-threatening stage 3 ovarian cancer in January of 2010. Now many battles later, I still have many battles left to fight, so I am asking for your support. No, not for me, but for all who are currently fighting, who will have to fight, and who have already lost the war with ovarian cancer. I feel I cannot just sit and do nothing. Feeling sorry for myself will not get anything accomplished. Being competitive in nature was distilled in me by my parents. Being of Irish descent, I know the stubbornness lies within, along with my "roll up your sleeves" attitude.

Writing my book *Ride, Baby, Ride!* was only the beginning. My family has started the Leilani Essary Hurles Ovarian Cancer Research Fund at MD Anderson Cancer Center in Houston, Texas. With guidance from my amazing oncologist and friend Dr. Michael W. Bevers,

I have set my goals to beat ovarian cancer. Please help me with our fight. Donations are being accepted at MD Anderson for the research fund. Envelopes and donation information are being provided by Kristine Shirar in the Development Department.

You may contact Kristine at
713-794-1084 or 800-525-5841.
Information is also posted on my website at
www.RideBabyRideBook.com.

No one knows where and who this "silent killer" will strike next. This is not only a fight for women. As with breast cancer, men can also carry the gene for ovarian cancer. Take time to research this disease and be generous by donating.

All donations go directly to the fund. You may make a donation in several ways.

1. Contact Leilani through this website and a donation envelope will be sent to you.
2. Make a check out to MD Anderson and specify the Leilani Essary Hurles Ovarian Cancer Research Fund on the check. Mail to:
   MD Anderson
   PO Box 4486
   Houston, Texas 77210-4486
3. Or contact Kristine Shirar at MD Anderson 713-794-1084 or 800-525-5841 for more information.

Every gift is a blessing and will help so many women in the future. Please give generously.

Thank you.

Sincerely,
Leilani Essary Hurles

Author of *Ride, Baby, Ride!* and
They're Pistols and They're Loaded

INFORMATION ON

Ovarian Cancer Signs and Symptoms

Ovarian cancer can sneak up on you. To protect yourself, here are signs and symptoms to watch for:

- Back pain
- Indigestion, heartburn, nausea, or gas
- Abdominal swelling or discomfort
- Pelvic pain or cramping
- Bloating or a feeling of being full, even after a small meal
- Painful, frequent, or burning urination with no infection
- Diarrhea or constipation
- Loss of appetite, unexplained weight loss or gain
- Unusual fatigue
- Shortness of breath
- Abnormal vaginal bleeding or irregular periods
- Pain during intercourse

Please remember, these signs and symptoms may be attributed to a number of conditions other than ovarian cancer. The most common tumor marker is a blood test called the CA-125.

A PERSONAL NOTE:

I was diagnosed with stage 3 ovarian cancer. I have always been physically active and never thought about the few symptoms I had. I attributed my shortness of breath, feeling full at meals, and a pain in my groin area—that seemed to go down my right leg…mostly at night when lying down—to my age (getting ready to turn sixty) and post-menopausal "leftovers." Please check with your doctor if you are worried or unsure about any of the signs or conditions that could be ovarian cancer.

HELPFUL WEBSITES:

www.cancare.org
www.cancer.org
www.cancer.gov/help
www.mdanderson.org
www.ovarian.org

HELPFUL BOOKS:

Bledy, Chris. *Beating Ovarian Cancer: How to Overcome the Odds and Reclaim Your Life*. Lake Placid, NY: Aviva Publishing, 2008.

Montz, F.J., Robert E. Bristow, and Paula J. Anastasia. *A Guide to Survivorship for Women with Ovarian Cancer.* Baltimore, MD: John Hopkins University Press, 2005.

Foods For Thought and Downright Good!

In every mother-daughter book, there has to be a recipe section. Just because! Family and friends are always coming up with good stuff to make the palate have an orgasm. You always hear, "I've got to have this recipe." Sometimes, you are lying through your teeth just to be nice because Aunt Matilda gets her panties in a wad when she gets her feelings hurt. But most of the time, it's a definite "I'm going to gain ten pounds and I love this *whatever*," and you do want the recipe. So Lani and I have come up with some of our favorites. Some from family… some from friends…some stolen…and some made up! They are usually made up when we get in the mood to drink a wine or two while cooking or baking. If the guys can grill and drink beer and Jack Daniels, then we can Merlot it right through a batch of cookies. And our lasagna is heaven with a little Chivas wine under the belt.

Have you ever taken a poll during the holidays as to who really even likes FRUITCAKE? I just know that every time someone opens one at either the house or office… everybody sighs a relief noise like I'm glad they got it and not me. I really have never figured out what is even in them. The dried fruit is totally gross. I could live with pecans and cake, but even the cake part isn't normal. I promise, in the recipes that follow, there won't be any "fruitcake secrets."

Lani and I cook with a different index than the glycemic one. Ours is more the "what the fudge" index! You really need to carry your ID with you to prove you're of drinking age to taste it. After all, we do our best work listening to George Strait and Dean Martin while diving into these kitchen sessions. As Billy Currington sings our motto: "We're pretty good at drinking beer!"

Michele Joy Polasek Recipes

Leilani's daughter-in-law, Michele, was cute and witty. If you verbally sparred with her…you were sure to lose! And though she passed away, we're sure she's haunting us now and wanting her famous recipe passed on.

Hangover Mac and Cheese

Caution…could burn down the house. Could cause loss of life and property. It's one of those OMG moments that mom-in-laws don't want to know about. Good thing son Dusty has an iron stomach!

1 box of Kraft Mac and Cheese
Follow box directions.
Drink excessively…pick your poison.
Wake up hungry and try to read directions.
Fall asleep and forget it is cooking.
Engage fire extinguisher.
Call 911 and insurance company
Gotta love your daughter-in-law!

Linda Harris Recipes

Linda is age sixty-six, eyes hazel, 5' nothing…weighs nothing. A brain at computers and math. Great friend, loyal like your Lab, and a good cruise companion. Likes Cape Cod cocktails and Coca-Cola (not exactly in that order)!

Linda's Hush Puppies

- 1 cup self-rising corn meal
- 2 cups self-rising flour
- 2 finely chopped onions
- Finely chopped jalapeno peppers (to taste)
- 3 eggs
- Salt
- Pepper
- Enough milk for medium batter

Mix all ingredients well. Drop by spoonfuls in very hot grease. Be sure to have a Cape Cod in your hand!

Frozen Sliced Sweet Dill Pickles

(This recipe makes very crisp, crunchy pickles.)

- 1 pound 3-inch unwrapped cucumbers, sliced 1/8 inch thick (about 4 cups)
- ¾ pounds 2-inch yellow onions, sliced 1/8 inch thick (about 2 cups packed)
- 4 tsp. table salt
- 2 Tbsp. water
- ¾ to 1 cup sugar
- ½ cup cider vinegar
- 1 tsp. dried dill weed

Mix the prepared cucumbers, onions, salt, and water in a 2 quart bowl (not aluminum) and let stand about 2 hours. Drain but do not rinse.

Return the vegetables to the bowl and add the sugar, vinegar, and dill. Let stand, stirring from time to time, until sugar has dissolved completely and liquid covers the vegetables.

Pack in Ziploc bags, seal tightly, and freeze. Makes about 4 cups.

Defrost either in the refrigerator or at room temperature.

Don't forget the Cape Cod! And don't let your mind stray with the cucumbers...ladies!

Angel Biscuits

- 5 cups sifted flour (plain, NOT self-rising)
- 1 tsp. baking soda
- 1 tsp. salt
- 3 tsp. baking powder
- 3 Tbsp. sugar
- ¾ cup shortening
- 2 cups buttermilk
- 1 pkg. dry yeast in ½ cup warm water

Mix all together. Knead well. Store in covered bowl in refrigerator. It's better if left overnight. Use as needed. Bake at 425° about 12 minutes.

Bake with a friend and get the kitchen really messy and don't forget the Cape Cods!

Auntie's Southern Boiled Custard

(Southern version of Eggnog)

- 1 cup sugar
- 1 heaping Tbsp. plain flour
- Pinch of salt
- 1 cup whole milk
- ½ gallon less 1 cup whole milk
- 3 whole eggs
- Vanilla

Mix sugar, flour, salt, and 1 cup milk together well. Pour the remainder of ½ gallon milk into pot and heat to a little more than warm. Add the egg/sugar mixture and stir well. Heat until almost boiling. Remove from heat and cool. Add vanilla to taste.

Pistachio Salad

- 20 oz. can crushed pineapple in heavy syrup
- 1 box instant pistachio pudding mix
- 9 oz. carton Cool Whip
- 2 cups miniature marshmallows
- Pecan pieces

Pour pineapple (juice and all) over pudding mix. Add Cool Whip, nuts, and marshmallows. Stir well. Does not have to "set up."

Pistachios and Cape Cods?

Patsie Lockett Recipes

Patsie Lockett is one of Lani's best friends, a party person along with her husband Mark, a Bud Light enthusiast, and she never turns down a shot!

Cheesie Potatoes

- 1 bag Ore Ida Potatoes O'Brien
- 1 can cream of mushroom soup
- 2 cups cheddar cheese
- 8 oz. sour cream
- Salt and Pepper

Mix and bake at 350° for 40 minutes. Don't forget the Vodka shots!

Broccoli/Spinach Casserole

- 1 box chopped frozen spinach, thawed & drained
- 1 bag chopped frozen broccoli, thawed & drained
- 2 sleeves Ritz crackers

- 1 lb. Velveeta cheese
- Butter

Put broccoli, spinach, melted Velveeta, and 14 crushed Ritz crackers in a bowl and mix together. Top with 14 Ritz crackers and dot with butter. Bake at 350° for 30 minutes.

Don't forget to have the guys grill a great steak with this. We can rent Patsie's hubby Mark out. He's the best at the grill. Must have Evans Williams (a Kentucky bourbon) available!

Zammitti's Italian Ristorante

Marinara Sauce

- ½ cup black ground pepper
- 1 cup minced basil
- 1 cup minced oregano
- 2 cups tomato paste
- 8 large white onions, finely diced
- 10 oz. water
- 2 cups granulated sugar
- 30 oz. peeled tomatoes (from can)
- 40 oz. ground tomatoes (from can)
- 2 cups olive oil
- 1 cup minced garlic
- 2 cups burgundy cooking winc

Sauté tomato paste, white onions, and garlic in small amount of olive oil. Crush whole tomatoes by hand and place all ingredients in large pot and cook until tomatoes are well cooked. Use immersion blender to blend to desired consistency, being careful not to splash hot ingredients on yourself.

Joe's Pinto Beans

Joe Frank is the husband of my good buddy Jenifer who lives in Belton, Texas.

- 1 32-oz. pkg pinto beans
- 1 can Rotel (tomatoes & green chilies)
- 1 large onion, diced
- 2 Tbsp. Lawry's seasoned salt (or to taste)
- 1 tsp. pepper (or to taste)
- 2 Tbsp. vegetable oil

Add ingredients to beans. Soak beans overnight in water. Bring to a boil, then simmer for around two hours or until soft. If you have a pressure cooker, the cooking time is approximately 45 minutes and the consistency is rich and smooth (this is my preferred method).

The Perfect Baked Potato

CREATIVE TOPPERS FOR YOUR TATOR!

- Olive and feta: 1 Tbsp. crumbled feta cheese, 2 tsp. chopped fresh herbs, and 1 tsp. chopped black olives.
- Salsa: 1 Tbsp. each of prepared salsa and Monterey Jack cheese, 1 tsp. reduced fat sour cream.
- Scallion Ranch: 1 Tbsp. low fat Ranch dressing, and 2 tsps. chopped scallions.
- Tex-Mex: 1 Tbsp. refried beans, 1 Tbsp. tomato salsa, and 1 tsp. chopped fresh cilantro.
- Creamy Horseradish: 1 Tbsp. reduced fat sour cream mixed with ½ to 1 tsp. of fresh horseradish.
- Mediterranean-style: 1 tsp. tapenade and 1 tsp. chopped fresh rosemary or parsley.
- Creamy chive: 1 Tbsp. pureed low fat cottage cheese, and 2 tsp. chopped fresh chives.
- Tomato Pesto: 1 Tbsp. prepared pesto, and 1 chopped small plum tomato.

These are suggestions given by Mountain King Potatoes. **www.MountainKing.com**. They are fun to try, and they make it fun at parties where everyone's taste is different.

Shrimp-and-Okra Hush Puppies

Creator unknown—always have to have a Whodunit!

8 servings

- 1 cup self-rising yellow cornmeal mix
- ½ cup self-rising flour
- 1 cup medium-size raw shrimp, chopped
- 1 tsp. Creole seasoning
- ½ cup diced onions, red and green bell pepper, and celery
- ½ cup cut okra, chopped
- 1 lg. egg slightly beaten
- ¾ cup beer
- Canola oil

Stir together cornmeal mix and flour in a large bowl until combined. Sprinkle shrimp with Creole seasoning. Add shrimp, onion, peppers, and okra to cornmeal mixture.

Stir in egg and beer just until moistened. Let stand 5 minutes.

Pour oil to depth of 4 inches into a Dutch oven. Heat to 350. Drop batter by level tablespoons into hot oil, and fry in batches 2-2½ minutes on each side or till golden brown. Drain on a wire rack over paper towels. Serve immediately.

About the Authors

Leilani Essary Hurles is a retired teacher and coach, mother, wife, author, motivational speaker, and a stage 3 recurring ovarian cancer survivor. She has devoted the last three years to uplifting spirits for those of you who just need a big hug.

Leilani has a BS degree in Education from the University of Houston. She currently resides with her husband, horses, and dogs in Fulshear, Texas. *They're Pistols and They're Loaded* is her second book, following the first *Ride, Baby, Ride!* She hopes her books bring hope and laughs to all battling cancer or any other adversities in life.

She continues her weekly Monday blogs. If you would like to begin your week with a good chuckle, visit her blog at **www.RideBabyRideBook.com**

Lani Dawn Polasek was born and raised in Houston, Texas. Lani graduated from Katy High School in Katy, Texas. She attended San Jacinto Junior College and Houston Community College. Lani has been caring for her mother since her diagnosis of ovarian cancer in 2010. Lani has recently moved to Columbia, South Carolina. She continues to talk with her mother daily and they are planning their third book.